THE RIGHT TO ORGANISE

A survey of laws and regulations
relating to the right of workers
to establish unions of their own choosing

Jay A. Erstling

International Labour Office   Geneva

ISBN 92-2-101790-7 (limp cover)
ISBN 92-2-101789-3 (hard cover)

First published 1977

Printed by Imprimerie Vaudoise, Lausanne, Switzerland

TABLE OF CONTENTS

INTRODUCTION

The principle of freedom of association is an integral part of the basic human rights which the International Labour Organisation has undertaken to uphold by fostering respect for them among the nations of the world. It was in pursuance of that undertaking that the International Labour Conference adopted in 1948 the Freedom of Association and Protection of the Right to Organise Convention (No. 87), a principal purpose of which is to guarantee for workers and employers, "without distinction whatsoever, the right to establish and to join the organisations of their own choosing".[1]

Although the principle of free trade union choice is widely accepted, its full application often gives rise to difficulties. It will be the purpose of this study to make a general survey of the situation by examining the relevant provisions of the laws and regulations of a number of countries and to consider some of the principal difficulties that have arisen.

In evaluating this legislation, reference will be made to the opinions on compliance with ILO principles and standards which have been expressed by two ILO supervisory bodies. One of them is the Committee of Experts on the Application of Conventions and Recommendations; the other is the Committee on Freedom of Association of the ILO's Governing Body.[2]

----

[1] Article 2 of the Convention. The text of the substantive provisions of Convention No. 87 is reproduced in Appendix D to this study. As of 1 June 1977, the following 86 countries had ratified the Convention: Albania, Algeria, Argentina, Australia, Austria, Bangladesh, Barbados, Belgium, Benin, Bolivia, Bulgaria, Burma, Byelorussian SSR, United Republic of Cameroon, Canada, Central African Empire, Chad, Colombia, Congo, Costa Rica, Cuba, Cyprus, Czechoslovakia, Denmark, Dominican Republic, Ecuador, Egypt, Ethiopia, Finland, France, Gabon, German Democratic Republic, Germany (Federal Republic of), Ghana, Greece, Guatemala, Guinea, Guyana, Honduras, Hungary, Iceland, Ireland, Israel, Italy, Ivory Coast, Jamaica, Japan, Kuwait, Lesotho, Liberia, Luxembourg, Madagascar, Mali, Malta, Mauritania, Mexico, Mongolia, Netherlands, Nicaragua, Niger, Nigeria, Norway, Pakistan, Panama, Paraguay, Peru, Philippines, Poland, Romania, Senegal, Sierra Leone, Spain, Surinam, Sweden, Switzerland, Syrian Arab Republic, Togo, Trinidad and Tobago, Tunisia, Ukrainian SSR, USSR, United Kingdom, Upper Volta, Uruguay, Yemen and Yugoslavia. Albania and Lesotho have withdrawn from membership of the ILO but remain bound by the Convention.

[2] The Committee of Experts is entrusted with the normal review and supervision procedure relating to standards laid down in ILO Conventions, including Convention No. 87. It annually considers the positions in law and in practice of the ratifying countries. In view of the importance attached to the question of freedom of association, the Committee on Freedom of Association of the Governing Body was established over 25 years ago to consider all complaints which are submitted to it, irrespective of whether or not the country in question has ratified the relevant Convention.

See, in particular, ILO: Freedom of association and collective bargaining: General survey by the Committee of Experts on the Application of Conventions and Recommendations, Report III (Part 4

(Footnote continued on next page)

The legislative provisions to be examined in this study are
those which: (1) regulate the structure and composition of trade
unions (Chapter 1); (2) result in the establishment of a trade union
monopoly (Chapter 2); (3) establish special requirements for the
creation of federations or confederations (Chapter 3); (4) create
systems of most representative trade unions (Chapter 4); and (5)
allow union security arrangements to be made (Chapter 5). Some case
studies of action taken by public authorities which may impair the
right of free trade union choice are given in an appendix.

It must be noted that the study describes the legal situation
in the countries reviewed and does not assess the practical
application and the effects of the legislation. Furthermore, the
legislative provisions studied are mainly those adopted prior to 30
April 1976. Many of them have appeared in the Legislative Series
which the ILO publishes at frequent intervals.[1]

(Footnote continued from previous page)

B), International Labour Conference, 58th Session, Geneva, 1973, Ch.
4; and Freedom of association. Digest of decisions of the Freedom
of Association Committee of the Governing Body of the ILO (2nd ed.).

[1] A list of the legislative texts used for the preparation of
this study is given in Appendix C.

CHAPTER 1

STRUCTURE AND COMPOSITION OF TRADE UNIONS

If workers are to exercise in full freedom their right to establish and join the organisations of their own choosing, they must be free to determine the structure and composition of trade unions.

The purpose of this chapter will be to examine various laws and regulations governing the structure and composition of trade unions, including especially those which deal with minimum membership requirements (section A), the occupational scope of union membership (section B), particular categories of workers (section C) and certain racial groups (section D).

A. Minimum membership requirements

The legislation of many countries provides that a labour organisation may not be established until it has obtained a minimum number of founding members. For example, in India, Malaysia and Singapore, as well as in some of the non-metropolitan territories of the United Kingdom such as the British Solomon Islands and Dominica, the minimum membership requirement is set at seven. Latin American countries frequently fix the minimum requirement at 20 or 25.

This is so, for example, in Bolivia (20 members), Colombia (25 members), Costa Rica (20 members), El Salvador (25 members for craft unions), Guatemala (20 members) and Paraguay (20 members for company-wide unions). A minimum of 20 members is also required in Ethiopia. On the other hand, there is no minimum membership requirement in, for example, Belgium, the Federal Republic of Germany, France, Italy, Sweden and Switzerland and in several of the countries whose legislation remains influenced by the French Overseas Territories Labour Code of 1952 (Chad, Madagascar, Senegal, Togo).

Legislation which sets the minimum membership requirement at a reasonable rate is not considered by the ILO supervisory bodies to be inconsistent with Convention No. 87. Often, however, the legal provisions fix the requirement at too high a figure. As a consequence thereof, the establishment of a trade union, particularly in small undertakings, may be considerably hindered or even rendered impossible,[1] thereby restricting the right of workers to establish organisations of their own choosing.

The Committee on Freedom of Association has expressed the view that legislation which, in one case, requires that a trade union must have "at least 50 founder members" fixed the minimum number of

----

[1] See ILO: Report of the Committee of Experts on the Application of Conventions and Recommendations, Report III (Part IV), International Labour Conference, 43rd Session. Geneva, 1959, p. 108, para. 31.

members "at obviously too high a figure".[1] A 50-member minimum requirement may be particularly burdensome, moreover, when the restriction applies to unions with a limited territorial scope or to those in small undertakings.

In Panama and in Somalia the applicable legislation contains a general 50-member requirement. In Nigeria, where a trade union may not perform any act in furtherance of the purposes for which it was formed unless it has been registered, the legislation stipulates that an application for the registration of a trade union shall be signed by at least 50 union members. Fifty members are also needed to establish a trade union committee in Egypt.

In some countries the legislation requires a minimum of 50 members for the establishment of a union of a specified geographic range. Thus, in Iraq not less than 50 workers in an administrative area may form their own union provided that they belong to one of the trades or occupations enumerated in the legislation. The legislation of the Libyan Arab Jamahiriya stipulates that a trade union may not establish a provincial branch union unless there are 50 applicants for membership in the branch and then only with the approval of the Minister of Labour and Social Affairs. In Nicaragua 50 members are needed to establish a union covering a departamento.

In certain countries the relevant legislation contains a modified minimum membership requirement. In lieu of requiring 50 founder members for the establishment of a union, the legislation provides that a labour organisation may not be created unless there are 50 workers in the same trade or enterprise. This is the case in, for example, the Syrian Arab Republic, whose legislation grants the right to establish a trade union committee to every category of workers in the same occupation comprising 50 or more persons. The trade union committees for each occupation and geographic area are in turn granted the right to establish a trade union. Thus, only categories of workers consisting of 50 or more persons may participate in the formation of a trade union. However, if several categories in a given occupation fail to satisfy the minimum requirement, they may join together to form a single trade union committee, provided that there exists one category of workers in the same occupation comprising at least 50 persons.[2]

In several rare instances, the minimum union membership requirement greatly exceeds 50 and thus may severely affect the right of workers to establish and join the organisations of their own choosing. In Kuwait, for example, there is a general 100-member requirement. El Salvador requires 100 members for the establishment of an industrial union. The legislation relating to employees in the public service in Venezuela likewise requires a minimum of 100 members. In the case, however, of a service with more than 1,000 employees, 10 per cent of them must be members of the union, so that the minimum membership requirement increases proportionately with the number of employees.

----

[1] Committee on Freedom of Association (see Appendix B, item 11).

[2] The Government representative for the Syrian Arab Republic indicated at the 61st Session of the International Labour Conference (June 1976) that the legislation on trade unions was being revised.

In Australia, a union may not be registered if its membership
is less than 100. Registration is, however, voluntary and gives
trade unions the right to participate in the conciliation and
arbitration machinery established by the legislation. This right is
denied to non-registered organisations, which nevertheless are
entitled to engage in collective bargaining and to call strikes.

What is, perhaps, the highest minimum membership requirement
is to be found in Uganda's legislation, which forbids registration
of a trade union unless it is composed of more than 1,000 members.
Unlike the Australian legislation which permits non-registered
unions to function, the legislation of Uganda requires registration
before a union can perform any act in furtherance of the purposes
for which it was created.

In addition to Venezuela (see above), countries such as
Uruguay and Turkey also prescribe a minimum membership requirement
in terms of a proportion of the workers in the trade or undertaking
concerned. In Uruguay the membership must consist of at least 10
per cent of the total number of workers in the pertinent industry or
establishment, while, in Turkey, a trade union must represent at
least one-third of the workers in the branch of activity for which
it was formed before it can extend its activities to the whole
country.

There are, however, also countries whose legislation requires
a minimum of 50 per cent or more of the workers for the
establishment of a labour union, thereby effectively precluding the
creation of more than one organisation in each occupation or
undertaking. This requirement, which appears in the legislation of
El Salvador (for works unions), Nicaragua, Peru and the Philippines,
will be discussed below in the chapter on trade union monopoly.

B. Membership confined to the same trade,
occupation or industry

Legislation very often provides that members of a particular
trade union shall be persons of the same or similar trades,
occupations or industries. Provisions to this effect exist in
numerous countries, including Argentina, Benin, the Central African
Empire, Chad, Congo, France, Gabon, Guinea, Ivory Coast, Jordan,
Kuwait, Madagascar, Malaysia, Mauritania, Senegal, Somalia,
Thailand, Togo, Tunisia and Uruguay. The Committee of Experts on
the Application of Conventions and Recommendations has commented
that, as the labour organisations regulated by such provisions are
often granted sufficiently wide scope to determine the categories of
workers they will cover, requirements prohibiting workers employed
in different branches of industry from "joining the same trade union
may be of a purely formal character".[1] This is particularly the case
when separate unions are permitted to establish and join federations
and confederations (see below, Chapter 3).

The Committee of Experts has pointed out, however, that "the
question of trade union structure ... is not only related to the

---

[1] ILO: Report of the Committee of Experts, 1959, op. cit., p.
104, para. 15.

general problem of the free establishment of occupational organisations but also to that of the promotion of strong and effective organisations" and that, consequently, "in certain cases the desirability of general unions (not restricted to workers of the same trade or occupation) may arise, especially in situations where industry is scarcely developed with a few small or medium-sized undertakings scattered throughout the country".[1] The laws of Colombia, Honduras and Mexico, for example, permit the establishment of general unions where the number of workers employed in each trade or undertaking is not sufficient to form a separate union.

In a number of countries, the legislation not only restricts union membership to workers of the same trade, occupation or industry but also specifies the industries or branches of activity within which the workers may organise. Provisions of this nature may raise problems of compatibility with Convention No. 87.[2]

The laws of the United Republic of Cameroon, Egypt, Iraq, Jordan, the Libyan Arab Jamahiriya, Sudan and the Syrian Arab Republic all provide for the establishment of a limitative list of occupations, industries or branches of activity within which the workers concerned may organise. In the United Republic of Cameroon the list divides the branches of activity into two major sectors, public and private, and further subdivides the private sector into several classifications relating to primary, secondary and tertiary activities. The members of each union must be persons employed in the same or in a similar branch of activity and not more than one union representing each branch may belong to the same central labour organisation.

The Ministers of Labour of Egypt, Iraq, Jordan, the Libyan Arab Jamahiriya and Sudan are empowered to designate the occupations and industries within which the workers may organise. Furthermore, in these countries the legislation prohibits the formation of more than one union per occupation or industry, thereby bringing about a system of trade union monopoly.

In the Syrian Arab Republic the legislation also creates trade union monopolies by forbidding the establishment of more than one union in each occupation. In that country, however, it is the Council of the General Federation which draws up the list of occupations permitted to establish trade unions.

C. Particular categories of workers

There are some legislative provisions which have the effect of restricting the right of particular categories of employees to establish and to join the organisations of their own choosing. These categories may include public servants and managerial and supervisory staff.

----

[1] ILO: Freedom of association and collective bargaining: General survey, op. cit., para. 65.

[2] See, for example, Committee on Freedom of Association (see Appendix B, item 33), where it is stated that "to establish a limitative list of occupations with a view to recognition of the right to organise would be contrary to the Convention".

(i) Public servants

As is clear from the terms of the Freedom of Association and Protection of the Right to Organise Convention (No. 87) and from the preparatory work which led to its adoption in 1948, the guarantees of freedom of association set forth in the Convention apply to employees in the public sector as well as to those in the private. The Committee on Freedom of Association has stressed this point by stating that Article 2 of the Convention "gives effect to the generally accepted principle that workers, without distinction whatsoever, should have the right to establish and join organisations of their own choosing" and that "this right applies to workers, whether public or private, and whether civil servants or not, with the sole possible exception of members of the armed services and police."[1]

In the legislation of a number of countries, such as Ecuador, Ethiopia, Jordan, Liberia, Nicaragua, Peru and Turkey, the right to organise is denied to all or most public employees.[2] However, even in countries where public employees are accorded this right, limitations of varying degree are frequently placed on the structure and composition of the resultant public sector trade unions. It is with this subject that the remainder of the present section will deal.

While permitting unionisation, the legislation of some countries precludes workers in the service of the State from forming associations jointly with workers in the private sector. Often, the purpose of such provisions is to prevent any form of political commitment on the part of the organised public sector staff or to dissuade any recourse to strike action.

The laws of Cyprus and Mauritania, for example, contain straightforward prohibitions against public employees adhering to unions which do not cater exclusively to the public sector. The applicable legislation in Switzerland guarantees the right of association to public employees within the limits laid down by the Federal Constitution, but, by prohibiting public employees from belonging to associations which contemplate or utilise strike action, in effect restricts their right to affiliate with organisations of private sector employees. In Norway an association catering for the public sector must be composed exclusively of government service employees in order to exercise the right of collective bargaining. There is a similar provision for the federation of such associations. Exceptions to the Norwegian provisions may only be granted in limited circumstances and by special authorisation.

The Committee on Freedom of Association, while indicating that it might be desirable to reconsider such requirements at an appropriate time, has considered that "a provision that government
----

[1] See Committee on Freedom of Association (see Appendix B, item 15).

[2] For an analysis of the right to organise in the public service, see ILO: Freedom of association in the public service (Geneva, 1975), pp. 3-13.

employees could organise only in unions catering for them exclusively may be reasonable in certain circumstances".[1] As in the case of legislation which confines union membership to workers of the same trade, occupation or industry (referred to in section B above), such provisions may be "of a purely formal character".[2] This is especially so when public sector trade unions may adhere freely to inter-union organisaticn.[3]

In addition to forbidding the establishment of joint trade unions, the legislation of certain countries restricts the membership of public sector organisations to employees of the same government department or of a specific class or group. For example, in Mexico an organisation of public servants must be confined to persons employed in the same governmental unit. Unions of public servants in Sri Lanka may not be registered, and thus may not function, unless their membership is restricted solely to persons employed in a specific government department or service or who belong to a specific class or category of employees. In Singapore a separate union must be formed in each statutory board or body designated by the Minister of Labour. The legislation of Malaysia requires that public sector unions shall confine their membership to employees within a particular occupation, government department or ministry. And in Pakistan the legislation provides that different organisations shall be set up for each category of civil servants.

The Committee of Experts on the Application of Conventions and Recommendations has considered that provisions thus requiring that a different organisation be set up for each category of public employees are incompatible with the right of workers to establish and join the organisations of their choosing.[4]

Some legal provisions impose yet another limitation on public sector trade unions. Besides confining union membership to workers of the same organisational unit, the legislation of a few countries also demarcates the labour organisation's territorial scope. Such provisions may likewise give rise to problems of compliance with Convention No. 87;[5] they are prescribed in the legislation of, for example, Japan and Venezuela.

The legislation of Venezuela provides that civil service unions may be constituted only at the national level. A separate organisation must be established for each ministry, autonomous

----

[1] Committee on Freedom of Association (see Appendix B, item 6).

[2] ILO: _Freedom of association and collective bargaining: General survey_, op. cit., para. 65.

[3] See below, Chapter 3: Federations and confederations.

[4] ILO: _Report of the Committee of Experts on the Application of Conventions and Recommendations_, Report III (Part IV), International Labour Conference, 48th Session, Geneva, 1964, p. 130.

[5] Committee on Freedom of Association (see Appendix B, item 15); see also ILO: _Report of the Committee of Experts on the Application of Conventions and Recommendations_, Report III (Part 4A), International Labour Conference, 58th Session, Geneva, 1973, pp. 120-123.

institution or other body whose staff is governed by the Civil Service Career Act. In Japan, a local public service labour organisation may not be registered or continue to be registered unless its scope is limited to only one local public body and its members are confined to the same class of employees. In the case of civil servants engaged in the field of education, a labour organisation may not extend beyond the boundaries of a prefecture. Trade unions which, through failure to comply with these provisions, may not be registered are not entitled to acquire legal personality. Consequently, they may not legally own buildings or property and may have difficulty in being recognised for collective bargaining purposes. However a Bill, intended to give legal personality to non-registered organisations, has been under consideration by the Diet.

(ii) Managerial and supervisory staff

The right of managerial and supervisory staff to establish and join the organisations of their own choosing is sometimes subject to special qualifications. National legislation occasionally contains provisions forbidding managers and supervisors to join or belong to trade unions whose membership is open to lower-echelon employees. Such provisions are enacted in order to prevent interference by employers in trade union activities and to avoid any conflicts of interest that may arise involving managerial staff.

Although such provisions thus serve a legitimate purpose, they nevertheless may come into conflict with the principles of freedom of association which are guaranteed by Convention No. 87 and which apply to all workers "without distinction whatsoever". With a view to reducing the risks of such incompatibility, the Committee on Freedom of Association considers that the definition of manager or supervisor should be restricted "to cover only those persons who genuinely represent the interests of employers".[1] The supervisory bodies of the ILO have further considered that, "having regard to the desirability of promoting strong and independent employees' organisations which can play an effective part in collective negotiation and the right of workers to join organisations of their own choosing", it is "important that the scope of managerial staff and the like should not be defined so widely as to weaken organisations by depriving them of a substantial proportion of their present or potential membership".[2]

The legislation of some countries contains a direct prohibition against managerial personnel affiliating with unions of workers. This is so, for example, in the Dominican Republic, Guatemala, Japan, Mexico and Thailand. In Sweden such a prohibition may be imposed by collective agreement.

----

[1] Committee on Freedom of Association (see Appendix B, item 23).

[2] "Report of the Fact-Finding and Conciliation Commission on Freedom of Association concerning persons employed in the public sector in Japan", in ILO: Official Bulletin, 1966, No. 1, special supplement, p. 504, para. 2202.

In the Dominican Republic the legislation provides that "no director, manager or administrator of any undertaking shall be a member of an association of employees", but does not contain any definition of director, manager or administrator.

The legislation of Guatemala stipulates that representatives of an employer or employees with similar status who, because of their high positions in the undertaking owe their first duty to defending the interests of the employer, may not belong to an industrial association of employees. Such cases of exclusion must be specified in the rules and must be referred solely to the nature of the supervisory positions in question and not to the persons occupying them. Furthermore, they must be approved and countersigned by the General Labour Inspectorate.

In Japan a labour organisation which admits to membership officers and workers at the supervisory level is not considered to be a trade union in accordance with the terms of the relevant legislation. Such an organisation may not avail itself of the machinery of conciliation, mediation, arbitration and adjudication of unfair labour practice established by the legislation. Officers and workers at the supervisory level are those who have direct authority to recruit, terminate, promote or transfer; who have access to information relating to the employer's labour relations plans and policies so that their official duties and obligations directly conflict with their loyalties and obligations as members of the trade union - or who represent the interest of the employer.

The legislation of Mexico deals only with employees in positions of confidence or trust and stipulates that they shall not be entitled to join the other workers' trade unions. It further provides that the labour organisations themselves may establish rules prescribing the status and rights of trade union members who are subsequently promoted to positions of confidence or trust.

In Thailand the legislation provides that "an employee who is a superior with the power to employ other employees, reduce their wages, terminate their employment, grant them rewards or discipline them may not become a member of a labour union established by such other employees or having such other employees as members". The other employees are also prohibited from associating with a union founded by "superior" employees.

Lastly, collective labour agreements in Sweden may, according to the applicable legislation, contain a clause prohibiting a supervisor from joining a labour organisation whose objective is the defence of the interests of those employees over whom he exercises authority. A supervisor is defined in the legislation as a person who is employed as a representative of the employer to direct, distribute and control the work which is performed by personnel subordinate to him and which he himself only occasionally performs.

Although the right to associate with lower echelon employees is denied in these six countries to managerial and supervisory personnel, they may form managerial and supervisory trade unions. There are, however, also a few countries whose managerial and supervisory employees are prohibited from organising even among themselves. This seems to be the case in, for example, the Philippines, whose legislation stipulates that "managerial employees are not eligible to join, assist or form any labor organisation".

A managerial official is one who is "vested with powers or prerogatives to lay down and execute management policies and/or to hire, transfer, suspend, lay off, recall, discharge, assign or discipline employees, or to effectively recommend such managerial action".

Regardless of how narrowly and explicitly the terms are defined, provisions which totally deny to managers and supervisors the right to establish and join labour organisations are considered to be incompatible with the principles of freedom of association guaranteed by Convention No. 87.[1]

Instead of directly prohibiting managers and supervisors from associating with rank and file employees, some countries provide that unions of workers may not represent or seek recognition in respect of managerial personnel. This is so in Malaysia and in Singapore, whose legislation stipulates that no trade union of employees, the majority of whose membership consists of individuals in non-managerial or non-executive positions, may seek recognition in respect of individuals in managerial or executive positions. The legislation also prohibits such trade unions from attempting to represent managerial or executive personnel for purposes of collective bargaining.

There are, furthermore, a few countries, including Malaysia, Pakistan and Singapore, whose legislation stipulates that an employer may require a person, upon his promotion or appointment to a managerial position, to cease to be and to refrain from becoming a member or an officer of a trade union of workers. In Malaysia, the stipulation also applies to "any workman employed in a confidential capacity in matters relating to staff relations".

As in the private sector, managers and supervisors in the public sector are occasionally prohibited from associating in labour organisations with non-managerial personnel. In some instances the laws dealing with the public sector clearly define which categories of employees are excluded from joining workers' trade unions. In others the scope of the exclusion is subject to negotiation between the public employer and the union. And in still a few others government authorities are entitled to unilaterally determine which employees are managers and which are not.

In Mexico the legislation concerning employees in the service of the Federal Government forbids individuals employed in posts of confidence to affiliate with trade unions of employees. The positions which are considered to be posts of confidence occur in the executive branch, the ministries, the legislature, the judiciary and a number of national institutions and commissions. They include the following: directors, deputy directors, chiefs and assistant chiefs of departments, offices and sections; inspectors; technical personnel; legal and technical advisers; labour conciliators; principals of schools; auditors; treasurers; supervisors and administrators of various types; and the secretarial staff of officials in posts of confidence.

In Singapore, just as in the private sector, public employees who are appointed or promoted to managerial grades may be required,

----

[1] ILO: Report of the Committee of Experts, 1959, op. cit., p. 104, para. 17.

as a condition of the appointment or promotion, to resign from membership in the trade union. A similar provision is contained in a draft ordinance dealing with government servants in Pakistan. The ordinance authorises the Government to demand that individuals shall cease to be or not become members or officers of labour organisations upon their appointment or promotion to supervisory positions.

In Japan the laws pertaining to national and local public servants provide that personnel holding managerial, supervisory or confidential positions may not form or belong to the same staff association as non-managerial, non-supervisory and non-confidential employees. If an organisation is formed jointly by both classes of employees, it will not be considered to be an employee organisation as defined by the legislation. The Act concerning the national public service establishes that the scope of the managerial, supervisory and confidential staff shall be determined by the National Personnel Authority. For the local public service, the competent personnel or equity commission is empowered to make the determination.

In 1966, the National Personnel Authority issued a ruling containing the list of positions which it considered to be of a managerial grade.[1] The list includes the following: heads and deputy heads of departments, bureaux and offices; councillors; division heads; secretaries of different types; room chiefs; office chiefs; branch office chiefs; sub-branch office chiefs; branch works office chiefs; and principals of schools and their assistants. In reviewing the scope of managerial personnel in Japan, the Committee of Experts on the Application of Conventions and Recommendations considered that "it should not be defined so widely as to weaken the organisations by depriving them of a substantial proportion of their present or potential membership".[2]

Lastly, in addition to the need, to which reference has already been made, to restrict the definition of public sector managerial staff to those employees who genuinely represent the interest of the employer, the ILO supervisory bodies deem it important, in certain cases, for governments to adopt "measures to ensure uniformity as between designations of personnel as managerial personnel and the like".[3] This requirement is particularly essential when, as is the case in, for example, Japan, the classification of managerial personnel is declared to be the task of numerous local commissions.

----

[1] Other regulations have been issued concerning local public servants.

[2] ILO: Report of the Committee of Experts, 1973, op. cit., p. 123.

[3] ILO: Report of the Fact-Finding and Conciliation Commission, loc. cit., p. 505, para. 2202.

D. Racial distinctions

In 1947, when the preparatory work on the Convention on Freedom of Association (No. 87) was taking place, it was clearly indicated that the right of all workers to establish and join the organisations of their own choosing was to be guaranteed without distinction or discrimination whatsoever based on race.[1] Racial distinctions, which are among the most serious obstacles limiting the right of freedom of association, are not frequently encountered in national legislation. The laws of some countries, moreover, specifically prohibit such distinctions. In Argentina, Japan and Turkey, for example, trade union membership may not be denied to employees on racial grounds. In the United Kingdom it is unlawful for a trade union to discriminate against an individual by refusing or deliberately failing to grant him the same benefits as are granted to other trade union members. In Canadian Provinces there is legislation on human rights and fair employment practices which prohibits discrimination in trade union membership. In the United States it is an unlawful employment practice for a trade union to limit, segregate or classify its membership on the basis of race, colour or national origin.

Nevertheless, legislation which imposes a system of racial discrimination on the right of workers to establish and join the unions of their choice does exist in certain countries. Thus, in Southern Rhodesia the system of discrimination is the indirect but practical result of the Government's exclusion of persons employed "in farming operations (including forestry) or in domestic service in private households", most of whom are indigenous, from the legislative protection granted to industrial employees. In the Republic of South Africa,[2] it is the legislation itself which directly creates racial distinctions and thereby prevents employees from enjoying, "without distinction whatsoever", the right to establish and join organisations of their own choosing.

The laws of the Republic of South Africa distinguish between three groups of employees: Africans, coloured persons and white persons. An African is legislatively defined as "a person who in fact is or is generally accepted as a member of any aboriginal race or tribe of Africa". A coloured person is defined in the legislation as a person who is not a white person or an African. Finally, a white person is legislatively defined as "a person who in appearance obviously is, or who is generally accepted as, a white person, but does not include a person who, although in appearance obviously a white person, is generally accepted as a coloured person".

----

[1] ILO: Record of Proceedings, International Labour Conference, 30th Session, Geneva, 1947 (Geneva, ILO, 1948), p. 570.

[2] For an extensive analysis of the trade union situation in the Republic of South Africa, see ILO: Apartheid in labour matters (Geneva, 1966): and Third to twelfth special reports of the Director-General on the application of the declaration concerning the policy of apartheid in the Republic of South Africa, International Labour Conference, 51st to 54th and 56th to 61st Sessions, Geneva, 1967-76.

Taking the view that it has not been found possible to fit the African population "living under tribal conditions and with a comparatively primitive stage of culture" into the legislative pattern of trade unionism and collective bargaining,[1] the Government of the Republic of South Africa has excluded Africans from participation in the general system of industrial relations. This system is established by the Industrial Conciliation Act which governs, inter alia, the registration and regulation of trade unions. In order for a trade union to become a legally recognised body corporate, it must be registered under the Act. A trade union which is not registered is merely a de facto organisation. However, the only unions which may be registered in accordance with the Act are trade unions of "employees", and Africans are excluded from the Act's definition of "employee".[2] Consequently, Africans may not join registered trade unions and trade unions with African members are legally unprotected.

The ramifications of this exclusion are significant. Because African workers are not considered to be employees within the definition of the Act, they are denied the protections and safeguards afforded to other workers who participate in the organisation and maintenance of trade unions. The Industrial Conciliation Act prohibits the dismissal or prejudicing of an employee because he belongs to a trade union or participates in its lawful activities. The Act also stipulates that no employer may require of an employee that he "shall not be or become a member of a trade union". No equivalent protection is granted to African workers desirous of forming or joining African trade unions. As a result thereof, as well as the result of other obstacles, most African trade unions exist under severely adverse conditions.[3]

----

[1] Statement by the Government of the Republic of South Africa in ILO: _Summary of reports on unratified Conventions and on Recommendations (article 19 of the Constitution)_, Report III (Part II), International Labour Conference, 36th Session, Geneva, 1953, p. 15. See also ILO: _Apartheid in labour matters_, op. cit., pp. 26-29; and Republic of South Africa, _House of Assembly Debates_, 1973, No. 1, col. 51, wherein the Minister of Labour stated, "... Bantu workers in this country are not yet ripe for trade unionism as we know it in South Africa".

[2] The Act defines "employee" as any person (other than an African) "employed by, or working for any employer and receiving, or being entitled to receive any remuneration", and any other person whatsoever (other than an African) "who in any manner assists in the carrying on or conducting of the business of an employer".

[3] For an analysis of the history and recent state of African trade unionism, see ILO: _Ninth special report of the Director-General on the application of the declaration concerning the policy of apartheid_, op. cit., pp. 8-12.

It should be noted, however, that no legal restrictions exist to prevent recognition by employers of African trade unions. Many such unions now exist and their number and membership is growing (see ILO: _Twelfth special report of the Director-General on the application of the declaration concerning the policy of apartheid_, op. cit., pp. 13-14). An increasing number of employers engage in collective bargaining with African trade unions, although their agreements are not enforceable, and strikes are illegal (though they have occurred).

The Government of the Republic of South Africa has established separate machinery for the settlement of African labour disputes. This machinery is contained in the Bantu Labour (Settlement of Disputes) Act, 1953, as amended by the Bantu Labour Relations (Amendment) Act, 1973. The legislation, which takes no account of African trade unions,[1] establishes a complex system of "liaison committees", "works committees" and "co-ordinating works committees" which lack trade union status and rights. The committees have no legal and enforceable barganing powers. They operate basically at the factory level and thus, for the most part, are not capable of ░░░░░░░░░ ░░░ ░░░░░░░░ ░ ░░░ ░░░ ░░░░░░░░░░░░░ ░░ ░░░░░ ░░░ ░░░░░ benefits, which are generally established at the industry-wide level for a given geographic area.[2]

Because Africans are excluded from the operation of the scheme of industrial relations as established by the Industrial Conciliation Act, the Committee on Freedom of Association has determined that "there appears to be discrimination with regard to the rights of African workers which is inconsistent with the principle accepted in the majority of countries and embodied in the Convention adopted by the International Labour Conference that workers without distinction whatsoever should have the right to establish and, subject only to the rules of the organisation concerned, to join organisations of their own choosing without previous authorisation".[3]

Significant restrictions are also placed on the freedom of association of coloured persons. The provisions of the Industrial Conciliation Act pertaining to the registration or the maintenance of registration of trade unions draw distinctions between white persons and coloured persons by imposing restrictions on mixed unions whose membership is open to both white and coloured workers. As from the date of the commencement of the Industrial Conciliation Act, no trade union may be registered "in respect of both white persons and coloured persons; or if membership of such union is open to both white persons and coloured persons". The only exception to this prohibition arises where "the number of white persons or

----

[1] On 20 February 1973, a Member of Parliament, Ms. Helen Suzman, introduced a private member's motion in the South African House of Assembly which stated: "This House is of the opinion that full trade union rights should be extended to African workers and requests the Government to introduce legislation to amend the Industrial Conciliation Act, 1956, accordingly." This motion was not accepted by the House of Assembly and the Bantu Labour (Settlement of Disputes) Act, 1953, as amended by the Bantu Labour Relations (Amendment) Act, 1973, ignores entirely the existence of African trade unions. During the Parliamentary debates concerning the African labour legislation, the Minister of Labour stated that it was "not in the interest of South Africa that Bantu trade unions should be recognised". House of Assembly Debates, 1973, No. 3, cols. 1027, 1071.

[2] For an analysis of the African labour legislation, see ILO: Tenth special report of the Director-General on the application of the declaration concerning the policy of apartheid, op. cit., pp. 5-9.

[3] Committee on Freedom of Association (see Appendix B, item 3).

coloured persons eligible for membership thereof is too small to enable them to form an effective separate union". In that case, the Minister of Labour may, on the application of the union seeking registration, authorise the industrial registrar to register the union in respect of both white persons and coloured persons.

Where the membership of a registered trade union is open to both white and coloured workers (either because the union was registered prior to the commencement of the Industrial Conciliation Act or because the union was granted an exemption by the Minister of Labour), the Act requires the establishment of a system of segregation within the union. The constitution of every such union must provide "for the establishment of separate branches for white persons and coloured persons; for the holding of separate meetings by white persons and coloured persons; and that its executive body shall consist only of white persons". In addition, the Act prohibits any member who is not an official or office-bearer of a union from attending in any union meeting "which is not a meeting for the particular race to which he belongs" and it forbids a coloured member to "attend or take part in any meeting of the executive body of such union except for the purpose of interrogation by such executive body or, with the consent of such body, of furnishing an explanation or making representations in regard to any allegations against him which is being investigated by such body". The legislation grants the Minister of Labour discretion to exempt such a union from all or any of these provisions for such periods and on such conditions as he may determine, but also empowers him to withdraw the exemptions at any time in his discretion. A mixed white and coloured union which fails to comply with the requirements is liable to cancellation of its registration. As noted above, a non-registered union is merely a de facto organisation.

When an application for registration is submitted by a trade union, an objection may be lodged by an already registered union. If the union which lodged the objection convinces the registrar that it sufficiently represents all or part of the interests sought by the union which filed the application for registration, the registrar may reject the applicant union's request or, alternatively, grant registration but limit its scope. If neither union is mixed, the registrar is accorded a great deal of discretion in determining whether or not to grant registration. He may deny registration to the applicant union on the ground that the existing registered union is already sufficiently representative of the interests sought, even though the applicant union has a greater number of members than the objecting union. However, if the already registered union is a mixed one, its objection cannot prevail and the segregated, applicant union must be permitted registration so long as its membership is more than one-half of the number of white (or coloured) persons in the undertaking, industry, trade or occupation and in the area. Thus, a mixed union receives less favourable consideration than an all-white or all-coloured organisation.

A distinction in treatment is also drawn if the registrar determines that the scope of registration of a mixed white and coloured union (i.e. the undertaking, industry, trade or occupation and the area for which the union caters) is the same as or includes the scope of registration of a union limited to white persons. If the membership of the white union comprises more than one-half of the number of white employees in the undertaking, etc., concerned, the registrar may vary the scope of registration of the mixed union so as to eliminate the mixed union's right to represent white persons. This provision of the Act also applies, mutatis mutandis, if the scope of registration of a mixed union is the same as or includes that of a coloured union. Furthermore, a mixed union whose registration has been so varied thereafter becomes liable to cancellation of its registration "unless cause can be shown to the contrary".

The Committee on Freedom of Association has recognised that legislation such has now been described draws distinctions which deny some workers trade union rights and prevent others from joining together in trade unions. It has therefore considered that such legislation is not compatible with the right of workers to establish and join the organisations of their own choosing.[1]

---

[1] Committee on Freedom of Association (see Appendix B, item 8).

CHAPTER 2

TRADE UNION MONOPOLY

A. Introductory

It has been shown in Chapter 1 that the worker's right to establish and join the labour organisation of his own choosing can be affected by laws and regulations governing the structure and composition of trade unions. More serious in its effects on the exercise of that right is the system known as trade union monopoly. There is trade union monopoly where the law provides, whether directly or indirectly, that there shall be only one labour organisation catering for a particular class of workers. Under that system, a worker may be compelled either to confine the exercise of his trade union rights to the single lawful association or to abstain from exercising his right to establish and join an organisation of his own choosing.

The purpose of the present chapter will be to examine three main forms of trade union monopoly:[1] monopoly at the primary trade union level (section B), monopoly at all trade union levels (section C) and monopoly through registration of trade unions (section D). It is, however, to be noted at the outset that the ILO supervisory bodies have considered that all systems of trade union monopoly imposed by law are at variance with the right of workers to establish and join the organisations of their own choosing guaranteed in Article 2 of Convention No. 87. According to the Committee on Freedom of Association, "this provision of the Convention is in no way intended as an expression of support either for the idea of trade union unity or for that of trade union diversity. It is intended to convey on the one hand that in many countries there are several organisations among which the workers may wish to choose freely and, on the other hand, that workers may wish to establish new organisations in a country where no such diversity has hitherto been found. In other words, although the Convention is evidently not intended to make trade union diversity an obligation, it does at least require this diversity to remain possible in all cases".[2]

Furthermore, "while fully appreciating the desire of any government to see the development of a strong trade union movement

----

[1] Legislation which imposes a system of trade union monopoly must be distinguished from that which provides for the creation of most representative trade unions. While both systems serve to avoid a multiplicity of employees' organisations, the existence of a most representative union does not preclude, as a general rule, the formation of a second organisation catering for the same category of workers. Consequently, systems of most representative trade unions are not necessarily contrary to the principles of freedom of association guaranteed in Convention No. 87. Such systems will be discussed in detail in Chapter 4.

[2] Committee on Freedom of Association (see Appendix B, item 26; see also items 7, 34 and 52).

by avoiding the defects resulting from an undue multiplicity of
small and competing trade unions, whose independence may be
endangered by their weakness, the Committee has drawn attention to
the fact that it is more desirable in such cases for a government to
seek to encourage trade unions to join together voluntarily to form
strong and united organisations than to impose upon them by
legislation a compulsory unification which deprives the workers of
the free exercise of their right of association",[1] and it "has
declared to be incompatible with the principles embodied in
Convention No. 87 a situation in which an individual is denied any
possibility of choice between different organisations, by reason of
the fact that the legislation permits the existence of only one
organisation in the sphere in which he carries on his occupation".[2]

B. Monopoly at the primary trade union level

The legislation of some countries requires that there shall
not be more than one labour organisation at the primary level for
all the workers in a given undertaking, public body, occupation or
trade, though such organisations are usually free to federate and
confederate. In some cases the legislation establishing this system
of primary trade union monopoly is in the form of a straightforward
prohibition to set up more than one organisation; in other cases,
the legislation prescribes percentage membership requirements,
thereby precluding the establishment of additional unions.

Provisions which outrightly forbid trade union pluralism at
the primary level are contained in the legislation of Colombia,
Honduras, Jordan, Mauritania, Mexico (public service), Panama and
Trinidad and Tobago (public service). In Colombia and in Honduras
it is unlawful for more than one basic or works union to exist at
any given time within a given undertaking, institution or
establishment.[3] If, for any reason, more than one such union does
exist, only the trade union having the largest number of members may
be retained, the members of the others being, however, admitted to
membership without further formality.

It is also unlawful in Panama to set up more than one works
union in the same undertaking. Where two or more unions do exist
they are granted one year in which to amalgamate. If they are
unable to do so, all but the largest union must be dissolved.

In Mauritania the legislation provides that "persons carrying
on the same trade, similar crafts or allied trades associated with
the preparation of specific products, or the same profession, shall
be free to form only one trade union" in each of these cases. The
provision further stipulates that every worker "shall be free to
join the trade union for his own trade or profession".
----

[1] Committee on Freedom of Association (see Appendix B, item 59;
see also items 22, 24 and 63); see also ILO: Report of the Committee
of Experts, 1959, op. cit., p. 50.

[2] Committee on Freedom of Association (see Appendix B, item 60).

[3] The simultaneous existence of a works union and of an
industry-wide union or of two or more industry-wide unions is,
however, lawful in both countries.

The recently enacted legislation of Jordan grants the Minister of Social Affairs and Labour the power to determine in which occupations, trades or industries the workers may establish trade unions. Only one trade union may be established for each category of occupation, trade or industry. In delineating the various categories, the Minister is directed to seek the advice of the Jordan Confederation of Trade Unions and to group the workers according to the similarity of their occupations, trades or industries, their interdependence or their contribution to the fabrication of the same or similar products.

The legislation of Mexico establishes a trade union monopoly for workers employed in the public service. The law provides that there shall be only one union in each government establishment. If another union is created, it may not obtain registration unless it represents the majority of the workers concerned. In that event, the registration of the first union is cancelled.[1]

A more restrictive situation exists in Trinidad and Tobago with regard to civil servants. The pertinent legislation states that, for the purpose of recognition by the Minister, an association may not be representative of any class or classes of civil servants already represented by an appropriate recognised association nor may it admit to its membership a civil servant who is a member of an appropriate recognised association. It would thus appear that, even if a category of civil servants already represented by a labour organisation were permitted to form or join other organisations, such organisations would not have any right to represent their members.[2]

In some countries the legislation is less forthright in requiring a trade union monopoly but the result is, nevertheless, the same. This is the case, for example, in Algeria, whose legislation requires the General Union of Algerian Workers to establish a trade union branch in each unit, enterprise or undertaking. The branch organisations are assigned the primary union functions of negotiation of collective agreements and presentation of individual or group grievances. While the legislation does not specifically outlaw the establishment of a second, non-affiliated association, such association would be, presumably, precluded from performing these primary union functions.

In lieu of a general prohibition to form more than one organisation, a number of countries require the support of at least 50 per cent of the workers concerned in order to establish a labour union. Provisions of this sort, which appear in the legislation of Bolivia, El Salvador, Nicaragua, Peru and the Philippines, likewise preclude trade union pluralism at the primary level.

In Bolivia and in El Salvador a works union may not be formed unless it represents more than half of the workers employed in an undertaking. In Nicaragua the support of 60 per cent of the workers

----

[1] See, in this regard, ILO: Report of the Committee of Experts, 1973, op. cit., pp. 125-126.

[2] See, in this regard, ILO: Report of the Committee of Experts, Report III (Part 4B), International Labour Conference, 59th Session, 1974, p. 146.

concerned is necessary to set up a trade union in an undertaking or centre of employment. The legislation of Peru requires that a union must comprise more than 50 per cent of the manual or non-manual workers in an undertaking in order to establish a manual or non-manual workers' union, as well as 50 per cent of both the manual and non-manual employees if the union to be established is a mixed one. And in the Philippines at least 50 per cent of the employees in the bargaining unit must be members of an applicant labour organisation if the latter is to be granted a certificate of registration, without which the organisation lacks legal personality and is denied the rights and privileges granted to legitimate labour organisations, in particular the right to engage in collective bargaining.[1]

In the USSR there are special legislative provisions concerning the rights of trade union committees at the primary level. Section 7 of the Labour Code of the RSFSR, which refers to the signing and execution of collective agreements states in particular that "a collective agreement shall be signed by a factory, works or local (branch or workshop) trade union committee on behalf of the manual and non-manual workers on the one hand, and by the management of an undertaking, institution or organisation, on the other". Section 230, which is more general, provides, inter alia, that "the factory, works or local trade union committee shall represent the interests of the manual and non-manual workers of the undertaking, institution or organisation in the field of production, work, everyday life and culture".

The Committee of Experts on the Application of Conventions and Recommendations has taken the view that these provisions do not contemplate the possible existence of another trade union organisation established by workers of the category represented by the trade union committee. The Government of the USSR has pointed out, however, that such a possibility is not precluded under the legislation which "only serves to reinforce the unity of the trade union movement in the Soviet Union which in turn is the result of an historic process", and that "the law confirms an existing situation". In the opinion of the Committee of Experts, "even if the workers of a particular category could set up a new organisation, the latter would not be able to carry out its functions since the legislation bestows these functions on the trade union committee exclusively". In this connection, the Committee, pointing out that the Convention requires "that trade union diversity should be possible in all cases", has considered that the legislation should be amended so that "should any workers wish to exercise the rights ... to establish other organisations to promote

----

[1] The rights of a legitimate labour organisation (i.e., one having at least 50 per cent of the employees in the bargaining unit as members) include the following: to act as the representative of its members for the purpose of collective bargaining; to be certified as the exclusive representative for the purpose of collective bargaining; to own property; to sue and be sued; and to undertake other activities such as co-operative housing, welfare, etc.

and defend their interests apart from the trade union committees, they may do so lawfully".[1]

C. Monopoly at all trade union levels

In an increasing number of countries, the legislation imposes a unitary system upon all levels of trade union structure. Thus, trade union diversity is prohibited not only at the local level of organisation but at the regional and national levels as well. Under such a system, usually only one primary organisation and one national trade union may be established for a given category of workers or only one federation for each category or region. These organisations may or must then affiliate with a single national confederation or trade union centre which is sometimes specifically designated in the law.

Examples of such unitary systems exist in several parts of the world.

A Latin American case is that of Cuba, whose laws expressly prohibit the existence of more than one works union in each basic unit, more than one national trade union in each occupational or administrative branch of activity, or more than one central trade union in the whole country. The legislation makes provision, moreover, for the establishment of the Central Trade Union Council of Cuban Workers to serve as the national trade union confederation.

In Africa, there are various types of legislation providing for a unitary trade union structure. The laws of Ethiopia, for example, permit the establishment of a single trade union in every undertaking employing more than 20 workers. Individuals who are engaged in similar activities in undertakings with less than 20 employees are allowed to establish a general union. Trade unions and general unions representing the same category of workers may unite in industrial unions; but no primary organisation may belong to more than one industrial union. All industrial unions may join the All-Ethiopia Trade Union, the national confederation which, under the law, "shall be the representative of all workers in Ethiopia".

The legislation of Sudan permits the establishment of one national trade union for each sector, industry or occupation designated by the Minister of Labour. Separate unions must be established for manual and non-manual workers and the creation of local union bodies does not appear to be authorised. The trade unions constituted in accordance with the legislation are permitted to form nationwide federations subject to the proviso that not more than one federation for manual workers and one federation for non-manual workers may be established.

The National Union of Tanganyika Workers is expressly established by the legislation of Tanzania. It is the only lawful

----

[1] ILO: Report of the Committee of Experts on the Application of Conventions and Recommendations, Report III (Part IVA), International Labour Conference, 61st Session, 1976, pp. 126 and 127.

trade union in the country and consists of several occupational branches. The functions and activities of the various branches may be co-ordinated by regional offices. According to the legislation, the President of Tanzania alone has the power to dissolve the organisation if he considers that it has failed to carry out its objectives.

The legislation of Uganda establishes a National Organisation of Trade Unions, which, the law stipulates, shall be the only central workers' organisation and shall be the association to which all lawful trade unions must affiliate. There are discretionary powers to refuse registration of a trade union (see below, section D).

Similarly, in Zambia all trade unions, only one of which may be established to represent a particular group of employees, must belong to the Zambia Congress of Trade Unions.

Several Arab countries have adopted similar laws providing for a pyramidal structure of the trade union movement with different types of organisations at various levels. The legislation of Egypt, for example, provides that the primary level of trade union organisation is the trade union committee and stipulates that there may be only one trade union committee for each establishment and in each city or village. A general trade union on the national level may be set up by the trade union committees representing workers in the same trade or craft, provided that not more than one general union is created to cater for a particular category of workers. Regional trade unions may, under certain conditions, be formed in the governorates by the individual general trade unions. The highest level of union organisation is the General Federation of Labour, to which all the general trade unions may affiliate. The General Federation is likewise authorised to establish regional federations in the governorates.

In Iraq, one trade union may be formed in each of the occupations or industrial sectors determined by the Minister. The unions are constituted at the level of the territorial district (muhafadha). One regional federation may be formed by the various unions within a particular district and one national trade union may be established in each profession or industrial sector. The regional federations and national trade unions must, in turn, be affiliated to the General Federation of Trade Unions, the national confederation sanctioned by the legislation.

Primary labour organisations in Kuwait, only one of which is permitted in each enterprise, undertaking or occupation, may group together in federations, provided that the federations are comprised exclusively of the same class or category of employees. Only one federation per occupation is allowed. A single labour confederation may be jointly formed for the entire country by the various trade unions and federations.

In the Libyan Arab Jamahiriya, the legislation authorises the establishment of one national union for each category, or for related categories, of workers. Each national union may, if certain requirements are met, establish one trade union section in every geographic district (mohafazat) and may also combine with the other unions to create one national federation. The formation of more than one association at any level within the Jamahiriya is expressly forbidden.

The legislation of the Syrian Arab Republic[1] authorises the workers in each of the different branches of occupations permitted to organise to establish one trade union committee. The trade union committees for each occupation and within each mohafazat may establish a district-wide trade union. A district-wide organisation is entitled to affiliate with its corresponding central trade union, which consists of all the other district-wide organisations representing the same occupation. It is also entitled to establish a regional federation, called a mohafazat workers' union, which comprises all the trade unions within the district. The General Federation of Workers' Unions, a national confederation, is specifically designated in the legislation to cover all the subordinate organisations. The Council of the General Federation of Workers' Unions selects the branches of occupations that are entitled to establish trade union committees, the occupations that are entitled to establish trade unions, and the occupations or groups of occupations that are entitled to establish central trade unions.

In certain Eastern European countries the law recognises only one central workers' organisation which covers all other trade union bodies. In Czechoslovakia, for example, the Revolutionary Trade Union Movement, which is cited by name in the Constitution as well as in the Labour Code and other legislation, appears to be the only recognised national trade union entity. The basic units of the Revolutionary Trade Union Movement are works committees. The right to engage in collective bargaining and to enter into collective agreements is specifically assigned to the Revolutionary Trade Union Movement and its basic units. According to the Government of Czechoslovakia, the references to the Revolutionary Trade Union Movement are given as examples and do not preclude the establishment of a second organisation.[2] However, in evaluating the legislation of Czechoslovakia, the Committee of Experts on the Application of Conventions and Recommendations observed that "even if the workers could establish other union organisations as explained by the Government, these could not perform any trade union functions as the law assigns such functions only to the Revolutionary Trade Union Movement and its basic units". Thus, "the practical effect of the law is to exclude any possibility of workers in a given category forming a different organisation".

The legislation of Poland requires all trade unions to be registered by the Central Council of Trade Unions, which constitutes the executive organ and one of the two supreme authorities of the Federation of Trade Unions in Poland (the other being the Congress of Trade Unions). The Federation of Trade Unions in Poland is itself described as "the body centrally representing the trade union movement in Poland". It would thus appear that every trade union must adhere to the Federation of Trade Unions and any new organisation which did not wish to do so would be refused

----

[1] See also footnote 2 on p. 4.

[2] ILO: Report of the Committee of Experts on the Application of Conventions and Recommendations, Report III (Part IVA), International Labour Conference, 60th Session, 1975, p. 104.

registration and, accordingly, denied legal existence as a trade union.[1]

It is of interest to refer, at the close of this section of the study, to two recent departures from the system of trade union monopoly imposed by law. In Portugal, where the legislation provided for a unitary trade union structure with a single central confederation, this system has been considered unconstitutional by the Council of Ministers and the question of its repeal is now before Parliament. In Spain, the special trade union system which existed under the previous regime has been repealed and a completely different trade union law has been enacted by the Cortes.

D. Monopoly through trade union registration

In addition to the methods described above, systems of trade union monopoly may also be established by means of the legislative machinery for the registration of trade unions. In many countries a trade union does not acquire a legal existence until it is registered with the appropriate government authority. The registration procedure is most frequently formal in nature and consists of depositing copies of the organisation's rules as well as a list of its officers with the trade union Registrar. The purpose of such a requirement is to ensure that the organisation has complied with the provisions of the trade union legislation.

However, in some countries the law "confers on the Registrar some discretion in refusing registration of a trade union ... when there is another registered union which in his opinion adequately represents the interests of the workers concerned ... or when he considers it is not in the interest of the workers to register a new union". Thus, while not specifically prohibiting the existence of more than one organisation for a certain category of workers, legislation of this sort is nevertheless capable of being utilised to bring about a unification of trade unions. Accordingly, the ILO supervisory bodies have considered that such legislation is likewise incompatible with Convention No. 87.[2]

----

[1] See ILO: Report of the Committee of Experts on the Application of Conventions and Recommendations, Report III (Part IV), International Labour Conference, 46th Session, Geneva, 1962, p. 97.

[2] See, for example, ILO: Freedom of association and collective bargaining: General survey, op. cit., para. 74; and Committee on Freedom of Association (see Appendix B, item 48), where it is stated that "provision entitling the Registrar to refuse registration to a trade union when he is satisfied that a trade union already registered is sufficiently representative of the trade or occupation concerned means that in certain cases wage earners may be denied the right to associate" and that "while it may be to the advantage of the workers to avoid a multiplicity of trade union organisations, unification of the trade union movement must not be imposed through state intervention by legislative means, as such an intervention runs counter to the principle that workers should have the right to establish and join organisations of their own choosing".

The laws of Kenya, Malawi and Nigeria, for example, empower the Registrar to refuse the registration of a trade union if he is satisfied that another registered union sufficiently represents the interests of the applicant class of workers. In Kenya, moreover, registration may also be refused if the other trade union represents a substantial proportion of those interests. In the event that registration is withheld, the legislation of all three countries permits appellate review of the Registrar's decision by the High or Supreme Court.

The legislation of Guatemala limits the circumstances concerning which a request for registration may be denied. The applicable provision stipulates that "for reasons of public interest and in order to avoid serious disputes between industrial associations", the Executive, through the Ministry of Labour and Social Welfare, may refuse to register or grant the status of body corporate to any industrial association if another association comprising more than three-fourths of the total number of employees in the undertaking has already been registered. In carrying out this provision, the Executive and the Ministry are required to "act in conformity with the strictest technical requirements ... [and] the democratic principles laid down by the Constitution".

The laws of Malaysia and Singapore provide that an application for registration by an association or combination of workmen in a particular trade, occupation or industry may be refused by the Registrar when another union has already been registered in respect of that particular trade, occupation or industry. Furthermore, where more than one union exists in a given trade, occupation or industry and the Registrar determines that trade union diversity is not in the best interest of the workers, he is authorised to withdraw or cancel the registration of all but one of the unions.[1] A decision of the Registrars of Malaysia and Singapore, unlike those of the Registrars of Kenya, Malawi, Nigeria and the British non-metropolitan territories, may only be appealed to the Minister of Labour. The Minister's decision is final and may not be called into question by any court of law.

The importance of the right to appeal to the courts against an administrative decision has often been stressed by the ILO supervisory bodies.[2] An appeal to the judiciary constitutes a guarantee against an illegal or unfounded decision on the part of the authorities charged with the duty of registering trade unions. However, the Committee of Experts on the Application of Conventions and Recommendations has pointed out that "when legislation makes it possible ... [for the authorities], directly or indirectly, to exercise substantial control ..., the existence of a procedure of appeal to the courts does not appear to be a sufficient guarantee; in effect this does not alter the nature of the powers conferred on the authorities responsible for effecting registration, and the

----

[1] The legislation of Malaysia requires retention of the trade union with the largest number of members; there is no similar provision in the legislation of Singapore.

[2] For example, Committee on Freedom of Association (see Appendix B, items 10 and 19).

judges hearing such an appeal ... would [ordinarily] only be able to ensure that the legislation had been correctly applied".[1]

What is perhaps the widest measure of discretionary power is to be found in the legislation of Uganda. Like the provisions described above, the Ugandan legislation authorises the Registrar to refuse registration if a registered union already represents the interests being sought by the applicant organisation. However, it also empowers him to refuse registration if the registered union is not yet, but is, in his opinion, likely to become, representative of those interests. Commenting on such provisions, the Committee on Freedom of Association has stated that "the power given to the Registrar to refuse registration when he is satisfied that an existing registered organisation is sufficiently representative of the interests concerned and, even more so, his power to refuse registration if in his discretion he is satisfied merely that an existing organisation is likely to become sufficiently representative thereof, appears capable of being utilised so as to bring about a unification of the trade union movement by legislative means". In the Committee's view "such an intervention runs counter to the principle that workers should have the right to establish and join organisations of their own choosing".[2]

----

[1] ILO: Report_of_the_Committee_of_Experts, 1959, op. cit., p. 108, para. 31.

[2] Committee on Freedom of Association (see Appendix B, item 48).

CHAPTER 3

FEDERATIONS AND CONFEDERATIONS

A. Introductory

To aid in the co-ordination, unification and centralisation of
their activities, as well as for added protection and strength,
trade unions generally join together in federations. Such
federations are sometimes formed on a vertical basis, i.e. by the
affiliation of various organisations representing the same or
similar categories of workers. They may also be established
horizontally by the adherence of unions representing workers in
different occupations or industries. For further unification and
protection, trade union federations, in turn, often adhere together
in confederations which may be national, regional or industrial in
scope.

The ILO has recognised the needs served by the creation of
such higher-level labour organisations in Articles 5 and 6 of
Convention No. 87 under which trade unions shall have the right,
inter alia, to establish and join federations and confederations of
their own choosing.[1]

While there are many countries where this right can be
exercised in full freedom, there are also countries whose
legislation circumscribes and qualifies that right. Such
restrictions have been held to be in contravention of the principles
of freedom of association, the ILO supervisory bodies having
expressed the opinion that trade unions should be free to establish
federations and confederations "as they see fit".[2]

It will be the purpose of this chapter to examine provisions
of laws and regulations relating to the right of trade unions to
establish federations and confederations and dealing with minimum
membership requirements (section B), the occupational or industrial
or regional scope of federations and confederations (section C),
prohibitions to establish a national central organisation (section
D) and particular categories of primary unions (section E).[3]

----

[1] See Committee on Freedom of Association (Appendix B, item 61);
ILO: Report of the Committee of Experts, 1959, op. cit., p. 115,
para. 72. These same rights are also granted to employers'
organisations.

[2] Committee on Freedom of Association (see Appendix B, item 61).

[3] There is an even more serious restriction where the
legislation authorises only one federation to be constituted for a
given occupation or region and where only one confederation or
national trade union centre is permitted. See the discussion on
trade union monopoly in Ch. 2 above.

B. Minimum membership requirements

In a number of countries the legislation regulating the establishment of federations and confederations contains some form of minimum membership requirement. The provisions generally apply to the formation of both types of organisations and require the affiliation of either an absolute number of lower-level organisations or a proportion thereof. Just as in the case of trade unions, minimum membership requirements sometimes hinder the establishment of federations and confederations. By requiring the affiliation of a large number of organisations, the creation of an inter-union body may be effectively impeded.

Some examples of situations where such minimum membership requirements are established by legislation are given below.[1]

The legislation of El Salvador requires the affiliation of ten or more trade unions to establish a federation. A confederation may be formed by three or more federations.

In the Dominican Republic seven trade unions are necessary for the formation of a federation and four federations for a confederation. However, the minimum requirement for a confederation is reduced to three if it is to be constituted by trade federations (federaciones de oficios). These requirements were established by the Ministry of Labour, which is empowered to exercise effective control over the formation of federations and confederations.

The legislation of Peru provides that not less than five unions representing workers engaged in the same type of activity may constitute a federation. At least ten federations are required to create a confederation. As most countries set the minimum requirement for confederations at a lower rate than for federations, the Peruvian legislation is unusual in this respect.

In Brazil, as in Peru, the minimum requirement for federations is set at five. However, the Brazilian legislation also requires that the founding unions shall represent the absolute majority of a group of identical, similar or allied activities or occupations. In the event that a federation already exists within a group of activities or occupations for which a new body is to be set up, the legislation protects the existing organisation by prohibiting the new federation from reducing to less than five the number of trade unions affiliated to the old. The applicable provision also regulates the establishment of industry-wide confederations by requiring the affiliation of at least three federations.

----

[1] On the incompatibility of such restrictions with the provisions of Convention No. 87, see ILO: Freedom of association and collective bargaining: General survey, op. cit., para. 120. See also Committee on Freedom of Association (see Appendix B, item 41), where the Committee observes that legislation "which requires the combination of no fewer than five trade unions in the same type of activity for the formation of a federation and no fewer than ten federations for the formation of a confederation conflicts with Articles 5 and 6 of the Convention".

To establish a federation or a confederation in the Philippines requires proof of the affiliation of at least ten subordinate organisations, each of which must be a duly recognised collective bargaining agent in the establishment or industry in which it operates. In the absence of such proof, the federation or confederation is denied the authority, functions and status conferred upon legitimate labour organisations which, as noted earlier in this study, includes the right to represent workers and engage in collective bargaining.

The legislation of Indonesia establishes not only a minimum membership requirement but a geographic requirement as well. In order to be registered as a labour organisation, a federation must have a membership of not less than 15 trade unions and be represented in at least 20 provinces. If the federation fails to meet these requirements, registration is also denied to its regional organisations, member trade unions and their respective subordinate units.

Lastly, in Nigeria the minimum membership requirements are not based, as in the above countries, upon the absolute number of organisations affiliating to the inter-union body, but rather upon the percentage of unionised workers that would be represented thereby. The legislation sets the minimum requirement for the establishment of a central labour organisation at "at least 40 per cent" of the country's unionised workforce. The applicable provision states that "two or more bodies each of which is either a trade union or a registered federation of trade unions ... may form a central labour organisation if, but only if, the total membership of all the trade unions concerned is at least 40 per cent of the total membership of all the trade unions for the time being registered ...". In addition, the registered offices of the respective trade unions may not be situated in the same State.

C. Membership confined to the same occupation, industry or region

The laws of some countries, including many with minimum membership requirements, confine the establishment of federations and confederations to constituent organisations of the same occupation, industry or region. Consequently, inter-occupational and/or inter-regional associations may not be formed.[1]

In most of the countries concerned, the law requires only that the component associations shall come from the same industry or occupation. Such is the case in, for example, Iran. In Peru the subordinate bodies must represent workers engaged in the same type or branch of activity. Federations may not be formed in Nigeria nor registered in the British non-metropolitan territory of Hong Kong or in Malaysia unless the members of the component unions are employed in the same trade, occupation or industry. In Malaysia, moreover,

----

[1] On the incompatibility of unduly rigid occupational or regional restrictions with the provisions of Convention No. 87, see Committee on Freedom of Association (item 64); see also ILO: Freedom of association and collective bargaining: General survey, op. cit.

the Registrar may, in his discretion, refuse registration of a
federation even if the above requirement is met. Lastly, the
legislation of Thailand permits federations to be formed only by
unions whose members perform the same category of work or who are
employed by the same employer.

Regional requirements are contained in the legislation of
Brazil, Nicaragua and the Philippines. The laws of these countries
contain occupational limitations as well. In Brazil the legislation
permits federations, which must represent identical, similar or
allied activities or occupations, to be established only on a state-
wide level. No inter-state federations may be constituted without
the prior authorisation of the Minister of Labour. Confederations,
the categories and titles of which are enumerated in the
legislation, may only be established on a national basis and must be
composed of the various federations representing the same activities
or occupations.

The legislation of Nicaragua provides that federations may
only be established by unions which function in the same
departamento. In addition, the unions comprised in a federation
must all possess a common characteristic; i.e. they must all come
from the same branch of production or the same undertaking.

In the Philippines, the legislation provides that "no
federation ... shall be registered to engage in any organizational
activity in more than one industry in any area or region, and no
federation ... shall be registered to engage in any organizational
activity in more than one industry all over the country". Thus,
federations must be composed of organisations representing the same
industry and may be established at the level of a particular region
or the country as a whole.

In at least one country the legislation concerning the
establishment of federations and confederations contains an inverse
occupational restriction: instead of confining federations or
confederations to organisations of the same occupation or region,
the legislation of the United Republic of Cameroon stipulates that
not more than one union representing the same trade or industry may
affiliate to the same central labour organisation.

D. Prohibition to establish a national
central organisation

While in some cases the legislation restricts the right to
confederate to the establishment of a single central organisation
for the whole country,[1] "there is also the somewhat opposite
situation in which the constitution of a national confederation
covering the workers of different industries is prohibited by law".[2]
This is so in Brazil. There the legislation confines the

----

[1] See above, Ch. 2: Trade union monopoly.

[2] ILO: Freedom of association and collective bargaining: General
survey, op. cit., para. 118.

confederations that may be lawfully constituted to those which are designated in the applicable provision and which correspond to specific economic activities.[1]

E. Restricted_rights_of_organisations_of_public servants_and_of_agricultural_workers

Legislative qualifications are sometimes applied to the right of certain employees' organisations to establish federations and confederations. In several countries the legislation provides, either expressly or implicitly, that such associations of public servants or of agricultural workers must federate among themselves and may not affiliate with organisations of the private sector in the first case or of non-agricultural employees, in the second. Such legislation thus subjects the right of public sector and agricultural trade unions to limitations not required of other organisations.[2]

In the case of public sector organisations, such restrictions are often the result of specific prohibitions against inter-affiliation. In Cyprus, for example, no trade union of public officials may adhere to another organisation unless it, too, is exclusively composed of such employees. The legislation of Malaysia prohibits a trade union of public officers from affiliating with a joint consultative, co-ordinating or other body unless the membership of all other affiliating organisations is likewise so confined. Trade unions catering to workers in the service of the State in Mexico[3] are expressly prohibited from "becoming affiliated to central organisations of workers or of peasants". In Norway a trade union federation or confederation will not be granted a right of negotiation if its membership consists of both private sector employees and civil servants. The legislation of Singapore provides that trade unions of public servants may not, without the prior approval of the Minister of Labour, affiliate with non-public sector organisations. And in Sri Lanka a union of government staff

----

[1] Brazil: authorised organisations include the National Confederation of Industrial Employees, the National Confederation of Employees in Commerce, the National Confederation of Employees in Maritime, River and Air Transport, the National Confederation of Employees in Land Transport, the National Confederation of Employees in Communications and Publicity, the National Confederation of Employees in Credit Establishments, the National Confederation of Employees for Establishments for Education and Culture, and the National Confederation of the Liberal Professions. These organisations may not amalgamate further.

[2] For a discussion of the right of public employees to associate in primary organisations with employees from the private sector, see above, Ch. 1, section C.

[3] This prohibition presumably does not apply to federations of public servants since the Federation of Trade Unions of Workers in Government Service is a member of the Labour Congress to which non-government service employees also belong. ILO: Report_of_the Committee_of_Experts, 1973, op. cit., p. 126.

officers[1] is prohibited from federating not only with private sector trade unions but also with other public service associations.

The limitation on the right of public service unions to federate may also be brought about by indirect means. Such is the case in Switzerland, where the legislation stipulates that public servants may not belong to organisations which provide for or utilise strike action, while, in Japan, a federation of public servants whose scope extends beyond the area of one local public body or beyond one separate category of employees is not entitled to registration and cannot acquire legal personality. Consequently, as in the case of a local public service labour organisation (see above, Ch. 1, section C (i)), it "cannot legally own buildings and property and might be in difficulty in being recognised for collective bargaining purposes".[2]

There are provisions limiting the right of organisations of agricultural workers to federate and confederate in the legislation of El Salvador, Liberia and Nicaragua. In El Salvador organisations of agricultural workers are permitted to adhere only to other organisations of the same kind, agricultural organisations being defined as those representing workers engaged in farming, cattle breeding and other related occupations.

The legislation of Liberia provides that "no industrial labor union or organization shall exercise any privilege or function for agricultural workers and no agricultural labor union or organization shall exercise any privilege or function for industrial workers". According to the Government of Liberia,[3] this provision precludes the affiliation of agricultural and industrial unions in joint higher-level bodies.

In Nicaragua the relevant legal provisions prohibit the formation of a federation composed of both urban and rural unions. Furthermore, the establishment of a confederation covering workers from both sectors is severely restricted. Rural and urban confederations may unite in a mixed confederation only if both the rural and the urban have a national character i.e. composed of the federations of at least eight departamentos.

In the case of organisations of public servants, the Committee on Freedom of Association has stated that importance has always been attached to the right to form federations grouping unions of workers engaged in different occupations and industries. Thus, the Committee of Experts on the Application of Conventions and Recommendations has pointed out that a provision of national law prohibiting organisations of public officials from adhering to federations or confederations of industrial or agricultural organisations seemed difficult to reconcile with Article 5 of

----

[1] A government staff officer is defined in the legislation as "a government officer who holds an office, the initial salary scale of which is not below 560 rupees per month".

[2] See, in this regard, ILO: Report of the Committee of Experts, 1973, op. cit.

[3] See Committee on Freedom of Association (see Appendix B, item 53).

Convention No. 87; and that legislation which permitted
organisations of public officials to federate among themselves and
provided for the official recognition only of such federations did
not appear to be compatible with Article 6 of the Convention, which
refers to Article 2 of the Convention with respect to the
establishment of federations and confederations and adhesion to
these higher organisations. According to these provisions of the
Convention, "trade union organisations should have the right to
establish federations or confederations of their own choosing
without previous authorisation".[1]

An exception to the above-stated principle may occur, however,
in the case of affiliation of public servants' unions with private
sector organisations "which contemplate or impose the use of strike
action". The ILO supervisory bodies have considered that, in the
case of public servants in essential services, "the recognition of
the principle of freedom of association does not necessarily imply
the right to strike".[2]

Limitations imposed on organisations of agricultural workers
wishing to affiliate with other workers' organisations are also
incompatible with the principle of freedom of association.[3] In this
regard, the Committee on Freedom of Association has stated that
"while the prohibition of a single union catering for industrial and
agricultural workers is not necessarily contrary to the Convention
... a government's refusal to permit agricultural unions to
affiliate with a national centre of workers' organisations
comprising industrial unions is incompatible with Article 5 of the
Convention".[4]

----

[1] Committee on Freedom of Association (see Appendix B, item 54).
See also, ILO: Freedom of association and collective bargaining:
General survey, op. cit., para. 119, and Freedom of association in
the public service, op. cit., p. 17.

[2] See, in this regard, ILO: Freedom of association and
collective bargaining: General survey, op. cit., paras. 109-111,
119; Committee on Freedom of Association (see Appendix B, items 2,
28, 49 and 57). The Committee on Freedom of Association has
considered that, where strikes may be prohibited for public
servants, "it is important that sufficient guarantees should be
accorded to them in order to safeguard their interests, such as
adequate, impartial and speedy conciliation and arbitration
procedures in which the parties concerned can participate at all
stages and in which the awards are binding and are fully and
promptly implemented".

[3] ILO: Freedom of association: An international survey (Geneva,
1975), p. 27.

[4] Committee on Freedom of Association (see Appendix B, item 55).

CHAPTER 4

RECOGNITION OF THE MOST REPRESENTATIVE TRADE UNIONS

A. Introductory

The legislation of a substantial number of countries distinguishes between the most representative trade union and all others. It does so by stipulating that only the union so designated is entitled to recognition by the relevant employer or employers' organisation for the purpose of collective bargaining on behalf of all the workers belonging to a specified category or employed in a specified work unit. The recognition of a workers' organisation is a necessary prerequisite in the negotiation process. To have fair and meaningful collective bargaining, moreover, the organisation recognised by the employer must have some degree of genuine representativeness. In order to resolve any doubts about trade union recognition, as well as to avoid the prejudicial effects of trade union multiplicity, the countries in which such legislation is in force provide that the organisation which represents either the majority or a certain proportion of a given category of workers or which has the greatest support in the case of competing organisations shall be granted exclusive bargaining rights.

It will be the purpose of this chapter to examine the various legislative systems and procedures for selecting the most representative trade union and for according it its special status and rights.[1] Consideration will be given to three systems of recognition of the trade unions that are most representative for collective bargaining purposes: recognition requiring an absolute majority of the workers (section B), recognition not requiring an absolute majority of the workers (section C) and recognition of several most representative trade unions (section D).

In approaching this question, it should be borne in mind that trade union "recognition" must be distinguished from trade union "registration". In the normal sense in which the concept is referred to in this study, "registration" is an act of the public authorities conferring upon an organisation the right to a legal existence as a trade union and to engage in those activities reserved for such bodies. "Recognition", on the other hand, is an acknowledgement by an employer or an employers' organisation of its readiness to deal with a trade union for the purpose of negotiating the terms and conditions of employment. It follows that registration, though it may be a condition of recognition, is not tantamount to recognition (except in special cases not here relevant).

The ILO supervisory bodies are of the opinion that systems of recognition which confer most representative status upon certain labour organisations are not, in principle, inconsistent with the guarantees of freedom of association set forth in Convention No.

----

[1] See also Alan Gladstone and Muneto Ozaki: "Trade union recognition for collective bargaining purposes", in *International Labour Review* (Geneva, ILO), Aug.-Sep. 1975, pp. 163-189.

87.[1] Indeed, the Constitution of the ILO itself incorporates the concept of most representativeness by providing in article 3, paragraph 5, that "the Members undertake to nominate non-Government delegates and advisers chosen in agreement with the industrial organisations, if such organisations exist, which are most representative of employers or workpeople, as the case maybe, in their respective countries".

However, the compatibility of most representative trade unions with freedom of association is not without limitation. In this regard the Committee on Freedom of Association has stated: "The mere fact that the law of a country draws a distinction between the most representative trade union organisations and other trade union organisations is not in itself a matter for criticism, provided that such distinction does not accord to the most representative organisation privileges extending beyond the privilege, on the ground of its having the largest membership, of priority in representation for such purposes as collective bargaining or consultation by governments or for the purpose of nominating delegates to international bodies. In other words, this distinction should not have the effect of depriving trade union organisations not recognised as being among the most representative of the essential means whereby they may defend the occupational interests of their members, organise their administration and activities and formulate their programmes, as provided for in the Freedom of Association and Right to Organise Convention, 1948 (No. 87)".[2]

Moreover, in order to ensure the rights of all the organisations concerned by avoiding any opportunity for partiality or abuse, the ILO supervisory bodies have considered it essential "that the determination of the most representative union should be

----

[1] See ILO: Freedom of association: An international survey, op cit., p. 17, and Freedom of association and collective bargaining: General survey, op. cit., para. 75. See also Committee on Freedom of Association (see Appendix B, item 25).

[2] Committee on Freedom of Association (see Appendix B, item 18). See also ILO: Freedom of association and collective bargaining: General survey, op. cit., para. 75, where the Committee of Experts on the Application of Conventions and Recommendations makes the following statement: "Where the law of a country draws a distinction between the most representative trade union and other trade unions for the purpose of avoiding the prejudicial effects of trade union multiplicity, this is not in itself contrary to the principles of freedom of association, if such distinction consists in the recognition of certain special rights - principally with regard to collective bargaining on behalf of a category of workers - to the majority union, that majority being ascertained in accordance with objective criteria ... This does not imply, however, that the existence of other trade unions to which the workers of a specific unit may wish to affiliate, or all the occupational activities of such other unions, may be prohibited. Such minority unions should be allowed to function and at least have the right to make representations on behalf of their members and to represent them in the case of individual grievances."

based on objective and pre-established criteria".[1] The Committee on Freedom of Association has pointed out that it has been regarded as essential in several countries that such criteria should include the following safeguards: "(a) certification to be made by an independent body; (b) the representative organisation to be chosen by a majority vote of the employees in the unit concerned; (c) the right of an organisation which fails to secure a sufficiently large number of votes to ask for a new election after a stipulated period; (d) the right of an organisation other than the certified organisations to demand a new election after a fixed period, often 12 months, has elapsed since the previous election"[2] In the opinion of both the Committee of Experts and the Committee on Freedom of Association, by providing for safeguards such as these, the right of workers to establish and join the organisations of their own choosing can best remain free of undue influence by government authorities and thus be truly unfettered.

B. Recognition requiring an absolute majority of workers

Several countries have adopted a rule granting most representative status to the union which represents the absolute majority of the workers concerned. Of these countries, it is perhaps the United States which has the most detailed legislation.[3] Its purpose is to eliminate or reduce the strife caused by serious and repeated recognition disputes. Under the applicable provisions, a quasi-judicial and independent government agency, the National Labor Relations Board (NLRB), is empowered to rule on petitions for recognition and to certify a trade union selected by the majority of workers in a defined unit as the exclusive bargaining agent for that unit. The NLRB is also authorised to determine the appropriate bargaining unit in respect of which the recognition issue is to be decided.[4] To perform this latter task the NLRB has developed a number of guidelines, paramount among them being the community of interest of the workers concerned (i.e. similarity in wages, hours and working conditions).[5] In addition, special provisions concerning units of craft employees and mixed units of professional and non-professional employees are contained in the legal provisions and administrative rulings.

----

[1] ILO: Freedom of association and collective bargaining: General survey, op. cit., para. 158; see also Committee on Freedom of Association (see Appendix B, item 43).

[2] Committee on Freedom of Association (Appendix B, item 25; see also item 58).

[3] Much of the law concerning the question of exclusive representation in the United States is the result of legal decisions by the courts and the National Labor Relations Board.

[4] According to the legislation, the bargaining unit may be an employer or craft or plant unit or subdivision thereof.

[5] For an elaboration of the bargaining unit guidelines, see Bureau of National Affairs: Labor Relations Expediter (Washington, DC, loose leaf), section 7, p. 47.

A crucial principle in the American system is that all decisions on recognition and certification as the exclusive bargaining agent are made by the rule of the majority of the workers concerned, expressed through secret-ballot elections held under the auspices of the NLRB.[1] This is so whether the workers are choosing between two or more unions, or between representation and no union at all. Where no absolute majority is obtained in the case of an election with more than two choices (e.g. Union X, Union Y or no union), a run-off election is held. In order to petition for a representation election, a claimant union must be supported by a showing of interest on the part of at least 30 per cent of the workers in the bargaining unit. The showing of interest usually takes the form of the presentation of authorisation cards signed by the bargaining unit employees.

A union which is certified as the exclusive bargaining representative is granted certain protections against challenges by other unions.[2] For example, no representation election may be conducted in any bargaining unit in which a valid election was held during the preceding 12 months. Furthermore, the execution of a written collective bargaining agreement of a definite duration bars a new election for a period of up to three years. The certification of an exclusive bargaining agent also imposes on the employer or employers' organisation an affirmative duty to bargain collectively. This duty is not only procedural, in that the parties are required to meet and discuss at reasonable times and exchange positions, but also substantive, as the standard of good faith bargaining depends upon whether the subject of negotiations is mandatory or not. The failure to recognise a union which has been certified by the NLRB is a sanctionable unfair labour practice.

A labour union certified as the exclusive bargaining agent is required by the legislation to represent all the workers - both members and non-members - in the bargaining unit. The terms and conditions of the collective bargaining agreement similarly apply to all workers. However, an individual employee or group of employees is accorded the right to present grievances to the employer at any time and to have such grievances adjusted without the intervention of the bargaining representative, so long as the adjustment is not inconsistent with the collective bargaining agreement then in force and the bargaining representative has been given the opportunity to be present at the adjustment.

The federal legislation of Canada reflects many of the same basic principles as that of the United States. The determination of the bargaining unit and the certification of the bargaining representative are the tasks of the Canada Labour Relations Board, a body composed of an equal number of members representing workers

----

[1] If, however, the employer commits serious unfair labour practices which interfere with the election process and tend to preclude the holding of a fair election, and the NLRB is convinced that the union would have represented the majority of the workers concerned, it may issue a bargaining order without holding an election.

[2] Thus, while recognition may also be voluntarily agreed upon by the parties, it is less often preferred to the formal certification after an election procedure.

and employers and headed by an impartial chairman. Employees
belonging to a particular craft or exercising technical skills may
constitute a separate bargaining unit. Certification will be
awarded to a labour union only if the Board is satisfied that the
union represents the majority of the workers in the unit and will
not be granted under any circumstances to an organisation that is
not fully independent of the employer. Although certification need
not be conditioned upon an election, the Board may order an election
when it deems it advisable to do so. If voting does occur,
provision is made for the holding of a run-off election in the event
that no union receives an absolute majority on the first ballot. A
union certified as the bargaining representative is protected
against challenge for the first 12 months following certification
and for the duration of an existing collective bargaining agreement
(not exceeding two years).

In Trinidad and Tobago, the system of recognition is not
unlike that of the United States and Canada. The suitability of the
bargaining unit is determined by the Registration, Recognition and
Certification Board. Many of the criteria applied are specified in
the legislation, including the community of interest of the workers
concerned, the nature and scope of their duties, the views of the
parties, the historical development of collective bargaining in the
industry or business and any other matters conducive to good
industrial relations. A trade union is certified as the exclusive
representative if the Board is satisfied that its paid-up membership
includes a majority of the workers in the unit. An election is not
necessary unless more than one union, as a result of dual union
memberships, claims to represent the majority of the workers
concerned. A union which fails to win recognition or which loses
its certification is prohibited for six months from reapplying to
the Board. The exclusive right of the bargaining representative may
not be challenged by another union for a period of two years
following certification except with the permission of the Industrial
Court, which must be convinced that there are good reasons for
waiving the two-year rule. As in the United States, there is an
affirmative duty to bargain in good faith and failure to do so is
subject to penalty.

Although somewhat different, the legislation of certain other
countries also accords most representative status only to the
majority trade union. This is so, for example, in Iran where the
legislation stipulates that, if the number of dues-paying members of
a particular union is greater than one-half of the total number of
workers in the relevant enterprise or occupation, that union may be
declared to be the majority union, subject to verification of its
majority status at least once a year by the competent authorities of
the Labour Ministry. A majority union is entitled to appoint the
workers' delegates to the dispute settlement council and to enter
into collective agreements concerning conditions of work and the
betterment of the workers' lives.

The legislation of Turkey stipulates that the labour union or
federation representing the majority of workers employed in a given
branch of employment or in one or more establishments shall have the
power to conclude collective agreements covering the branch or
establishments in question. Workers who do not belong to the most
representative union, however, may not avail themselves of the
collective agreement unless they pay a monthly solidarity
contribution to the union concerned. The rate of payment may not

exceed two-thirds of the union membership dues paid by workers of the same class and skill who work in the same establishment. The manner of paying the contribution may be determined by each organisation. The legislation provides, furthermore, for the extension of labour agreements.[1]

In El Salvador a union must represent at least 51 per cent of the workers in an undertaking or establishment for the purpose of exclusive negotiation of a collective bargaining agreement. A union which loses its 51 per cent majority also loses its right to serve as the exclusive representative and may be replaced by another organisation if that organisation obtains the required percentage. If two or more unions exist in the same enterprise or undertaking and no single union possesses the necessary majority, all the unions may join together for the purpose of obtaining it. If together they represent 51 per cent of the total workforce, they are granted the right to negotiate jointly a collective agreement. In addition to outlining the procedure for the selection of the bargaining representative, the legislation imposes on the employer an affirmative duty to bargain.

The legislation of Colombia stipulates that, where a basic (works) union exists side by side with a trade or industrial union in the same undertaking, the workers shall be represented for all collective bargaining purposes by the union to which the "clear majority" of them belong.[2] However, the minority union or unions may submit a list of desired bargaining demands to the bargaining representative. The representative is obliged to present the minority unions' demands to the employer if they are approved by a majority of the participants at a general union meeting which it is the duty of the majority representative to call. Furthermore, if 75 per cent or more of the workers employed in a particular trade or having a particular skill are members of the same union, that union is granted the right to bargain directly with the employer and any decisions reached must form a separate chapter of the over-all collective bargaining agreement. Where there is no single majority union in an undertaking, the list of bargaining demands is generally drafted by all the organisations and the workers are represented jointly by a bargaining committee, the composition of which must reflect the number of workers belonging to each union.

The recently enacted legislation of Jamaica provides that, "if there is any doubt or dispute: (a) as to whether the workers, or a particular category of the workers, in the employment of an employer wish any, and if so which, trade union to have bargaining rights in relation to them; cr (b) as to which of two or more trade unions claiming bargaining rights in relation to such workers or category

----

[1] An extendable labour agreement is one whose scope may be broadened to cover all employers and employees (including non-members of the organisations negotiating the agreement) in the industry or branch of activity for which it was negotiated. The concept of extension is a common one and is provided for in the legislation of many other countries, including several of those mentioned in this chapter.

[2] The legislation outlaws the existence of two or more basic unions in the same undertaking. See above, Ch. 2: Trade union monopoly.

of workers should be recognised as having such bargaining rights",
the Minister of Labour "may cause a ballot of such workers or
categories of workers to be taken for the purpose of determining the
matter". The Minister is also authorised to settle any disagreement
regarding the ballot. In the event that he is unable to resolve
such a disagreement, he may refer it to the Industrial Disputes
Tribunal for a determination. If the results of the election
indicate that the majority of all workers eligible to participate
therein voted in favour of granting bargaining rights to a
particular trade union, the employer is obliged to recognise it as
the exclusive bargaining representative. Where, however, the choice
is between two or more trade unions and the results show that each
of two or three of those received the votes of not less than 30 per
cent of all workers eligible to vote, joint bargaining rights, as in
El Salvador or in Colombia, may be granted, so long as at least two
of the unions so desire. Any person who prevents an eligible worker
from voting or an employer who fails to recognise a union granted
bargaining rights is in violation of the legislation and guilty of
an offence.

C. Recognition not requiring an absolute majority of workers

There are also countries whose legislation, unlike that of the
countries referred to in section B above, does not require an
absolute majority of workers in order to entitle a trade union to
recognition and to serve as the exclusive bargaining agent.

The legislation of Pakistan provides that, where only one
registered trade union operates in an enterprise or a group of
enterprises and its membership comprises one-third or more of the
workers, it must be recognised as the collective bargaining
representative. Where there is more than one registered union with
a membership of one-third or more of the workers, the Registrar is
empowered, upon the application of any of the unions concerned, to
hold a secret ballot. All registered unions[1] may compete in the
election and all members of any of the competing unions may vote,
non-union members being, however, prohibited from voting. The trade
union which receives the highest number of votes, but provided that
the number equals at least one-third of all those employed in the
enterprise or enterprises concerned, must be recognised as the
collective bargaining agent. This status is protected for a period
of two years. Only the collective bargaining agent is entitled to
enter into agreements on behalf of the workers concerned and any
labour agreement reached between it and the employer is binding on
all the employees. On the other hand, no agreement may be concluded
between the employer and a union other than the collective
bargaining agent. In addition, representation before labour courts
is limited to the collective bargaining agent or to the worker
himself.
----

[1] In order to check an undue proliferation of trade unions, the
amending legislation of 1975 provides that, in an establishment
where two registered trade unions already exist, no other trade
union may be registered unless its membership includes at least 20
per cent of the total number of workers employed therein.

To determine the collective bargaining agents among industry-wide trade unions, the federations of such organisations and federations at the national level, the Pakistani legislation establishes a National Industrial Relations Commission. However, the legislation sets no standards for the determination of such bargaining status. The role of the Commission is, in any event, unclear as collective bargaining in Pakistan remains primarily an enterprise or local matter.

In Mexico, an employer is under a legal obligation to recognise a trade union and negotiate with it. Consequently, where only one trade union exists in an enterprise, it serves as the bargaining representative regardless of the size of its membership. Where there is more than one union in the same undertaking, recognition must be granted to the one with the largest number of members employed in that undertaking. The determination of the union with the largest membership is made by conciliation and arbitration boards which are tripartite bodies established at the federal and state levels.

In certain instances, craft unions in Mexico may be granted separate recognition for bargaining. Where several trades are employed in the same undertaking, the craft unions representing the largest numbers of workers in each trade may agree to form a joint negotiating panel. If they choose not to do so, each union may be recognised for the trade it represents. Furthermore, if craft unions coexist with enterprise or industrial unions in the same undertaking, each craft union may be designated as the bargaining representative for its particular trade, provided that its membership is larger than the number of workers in the same trade belonging to other unions. A union loses its right of exclusive representation if the conciliation and arbitration board concerned certifies that it has ceased to have the largest membership.

A comparable system of representation exists in Honduras. Under the applicable legislation, every person employing workers belonging to a trade union is required to conclude a collective agreement with that trade union if it so requests. If two or more trade unions exist in an undertaking,[1] the agreement must be made with the union having the largest number of members. In addition, the agreement may not contain provisions less favourable to the workers than those contained in the agreement already in force in the undertaking.

Similarly, in Ecuador every employer who employs 15 or more employees belonging to an association is bound to conclude a collective agreement if the association so requests. Where there is a works council, the constituent meeting of which must comprise over 50 per cent of the undertaking's employees, its managing committee is responsible for representing all the employees in the collective agreement. However, if two or more associations (other than works councils) exist in the same undertaking, the employer must negotiate with the association to which the greatest number of employees belong. Furthermore, as in Mexico, employees working in the same

----

[1] This provision seems to refer to the joint existence in the same undertaking of a works union and an industry-wide union or two or more industry-wide unions, as the existence of two works unions is forbidden by law (see above, Ch. 2: Trade union monopoly).

undertaking belonging to different occupational groups are accorded the right to have separate bargaining representatives. If the various representatives so desire, they may negotiate a joint agreement with the employer. In the alternative, the employer is required to conclude a separate contract with each occupational association.

The legislation of Costa Rica compels an employer to negotiate with a labour organisation whose members comprise at least one-third of the employees in a given undertaking, or one-third of those employed in a particular establishment if the undertaking concerned carries on work in different districts of the country. Where two or more unions meet this requirement, the right to negotiate the collective agreement is granted to the union with the greatest number of members. In addition, a provision similar to that of Mexico and Ecuador exists in the case of an undertaking or establishment which, owing to the nature of its operation, employs persons belonging to different occupations or trades.

The legislation of Argentina is intended to consolidate trade unions with a broad organisational scope by means of a system which accords extensive power to the most representative union. According to the applicable provisions, a most representative occupational association of workers is one which "has the largest number of members and such number giving it sufficient authority to represent the activity or category concerned in its area of operation ... [and] has been in operation as an occupational association for more than six months". Where a most representative occupational association with special status for the trade (personería gremial) already exists, that status may not be granted to another association for the same area and activity "unless the number of dues-paying members belonging to the latter over a continuous period of at least six months immediately prior to its application was appreciably greater than the number belonging to the association already enjoying such status. Where an occupational association of workers is a general or an industry-wide association or trade union and the association applying for trade status is a union for a particular craft, occupation or category, the latter will be deemed to be the most representative only if its occupational interests "are so fundamentally different from those encountered in the activity covered by the former as to warrant specific representation". Thus, contrary to the system in the other Latin American countries referred to above, craft or occupational unions are treated less favourably than associations with a broader organisational scope. Nor may most representative status be granted to a trade union which is limited to a given undertaking or establishment unless there is no first-degree organisation, general union or second-degree organisation already designated as most representative for the activity concerned. Furthermore, where a first-degree organisation desires to represent a certain activity in a specific area, it may be selected to do so only if there is no other organisation of the same degree or a general union with power to represent the same activity over an appreciably wider area.

The unions which are legislatively distinguished in Argentina as the most representative for the trade and which are endowed with special status (personería gremial) enjoy a number of exclusive rights. Included among these are the following: to defend and represent, vis-à-vis the State and the employers, the collective and individual occupational interests of the workers on whose behalf the organisations operate; to defend and represent the personal interests of their members vis-à-vis the social security institutions, courts of law and other public bodies; to participate in the work of the public bodies concerned with the regulation of labour and social security and to assist in supervising the enforcement of social legislation; to engage in collective bargaining and to conclude and modify collective agreements; to use the words "trade union" or "general union" in their titles; to support political parties; and to hold meetings in private without the requirement to obtain prior permission. By limiting the conferral of such rights to unions with special legal personality for the trade, the legislation of Argentina goes further than that of the other countries that have been considered in distinguishing between most representative unions and all others.[1]

The legislation of Nigeria is special in that it requires a qualified majority status only in a situation of rival unions. In the absence of a rival union a claimant organisation is entitled to recognition by an employer regardless of the number of employees it represents. If the employer refuses to recognise the union, a compulsory recognition order may be issued by the Commissioner of Labour. Failure to comply with such an order makes the employer liable to penalty. A recognised union may continue to enjoy such status until it is challenged by another organisation asserting membership among the same group of workers. In that event the employer is required to recognise only the union whose membership includes 60 per cent or more of the workers concerned. Disputes concerning the satisfaction of the 60 per cent requirement are settled by the Commissioner, who is authorised to enforce his decision with a compulsory recognition order. Thereafter, the employer may apply to the Commissioner for a determination that, over a six-month period since recognition was granted, the membership of the recognised union has fallen below the 60 per cent minimum. If the Commissioner so determines, the union concerned ceases to be entitled to recognition as of right. The Commissioner may also refuse to issue a compulsory recognition order although a union represents 60 per cent or more of the workforce, in which case the union is not entitled to recognition by the employer for a period of one year from the date of the refusal.

Finally, in the United Kingdom recognition has, as a general rule, been traditionally granted on an exclusive basis but has only recently been the subject of legislation. The Industrial Relations Act of 1971 for the first time introduced the notions of "bargaining units" and "sole bargaining agents" into the annals of British law. Although the Industrial Relations Act was subsequently repealed and replaced by the Trade Union and Labour Relations Act of 1974, as amended by the Trade Union and Labour Relations (Amendment) Act, 1976, its companion Industrial Relations Code of Practice remained in effect. According to the Code, an employer, when faced with a demand for recognition, is advised to take into account the extent of support for the claimant union among the workers concerned, the effect of granting recognition on any existing bargaining agreements, and the question whether the representation unit should include supervisors as well as those supervised. The Code places responsibility for avoiding recognition disputes between unions on
----

[1] See ILO: Report of the Committee of Experts, 1975, op. cit., pp. 100, 101.

the unions themselves and also on the Trades Union Congress, the national central organisation. According to the 1974 legislation, as amended, failure to abide by a provision of a Code of Practice is not an actionable offence but the provisions of any such Code of Practice are admissible in evidence in any proceedings before an industrial tribunal and may be taken into account by that tribunal.

The recently enacted Employment Protection Act of 1975 lays down a procedure for dealing with questions of recognition. An independent trade union, i.e. one which is neither dominated nor controlled by employers, may refer an issue of recognition by an employer for the purpose of collective bargaining to the Advisory, Conciliation and Arbitration Service (ACAS). The ACAS is required to seek to assist a settlement of the recognition issue by conciliation. In so doing, it is authorised to examine the issue, consult all parties who, it considers, will be affected by the outcome of the reference and make such inquiries as it thinks fit, including ascertainment of the opinions of workers by taking a formal ballot or by other means.

If the issue has not been settled by conciliation, the ACAS must prepare a written report setting out its findings, its advice and any recommendation for recognition and the reasons for it, or, where no such recommendation is made, the reasons for not making one. The ACAS may subject a recommendation for recognition to such conditions, to be complied with on the part of the trade union, as it thinks fit. An unconditional recommendation for recognition becomes operative 14 days from the date on which it was reported to the employer and, in the case of a conditional recommendation, 14 days from the date on which the ACAS advises the employer that the conditions have been complied with by the union. The recommendation remains operative until it has been superseded by an express or implied agreement between the employer and the union, replaced by another recommendation or revoked.

If an employer fails to comply with a recommendation for recognition for a period of two months following the date on which such recommendation became operative, the trade union concerned may lodge a complaint with the ACAS. (An employer is "not complying with" a recommendation when, at the time of the complaint, "he is not then taking such action by way of or with a view to carrying on negotiations as might reasonably be expected to be taken by an employer ready and willing to carry on such negotiations as are envisaged by the recommendation".) The ACAS must try to settle the matter by conciliation; but, if conciliation does not result in a settlement, the trade union may refer its complaint to the Central Arbitration Committee, indicating the terms and conditions that it desires to have included in the contracts of the employees covered by the ACAS recommendation. If, after hearing the parties, the Committee determines that the complaint is well founded, it may make an award directing the employer to observe either the terms and conditions specified in the trade union's claim or any other terms and conditions which it considers appropriate. The Committee's award may be superseded or varied by a subsequent collective bargaining agreement.

D. Recognition of several most representative
trade unions

As the term has been used in this chapter, a most
representative trade union is synonymous with an exclusive
bargaining agent. However, in certain countries recognition is
granted on a non-exclusive basis with the result that there may be
a number of most representative trade unions bargaining for the same
group of workers. This is particularly so in Belgium and France,
where collective bargaining very often takes place on an industry-
wide level and where the trade union movement is divided along
ideological or political lines.

A union designated as representative in Belgium is granted the
right to be a member of the statutory industry joint committees
which are responsible for the bulk of the collective negotiations.
According to Belgian legislation, the conditions for enjoying
representative status require that an organisation be inter-
occupational in scope, contain at least 50,000 members and be
represented on the Central Economic Council and the National Labour
Council, or that it be affiliated to such an inter-occupational
organisation. From among the organisations which meet these
requirements, the Minister responsible for labour affairs may
designate the members of the joint negotiating committees and
determine their relative voting strength.

In France the relevant legislation cites membership,
independence, amount of dues, years of experience and patriotic
attitude during the Second World War as the criteria for selecting
the most representative unions eligible to negotiate collective
agreements subject to extension. The meetings for the negotiation
of such agreements are convened by the Labour Minister at the
request of the most representative unions. The relevant employers'
organisations may be obliged by law to attend. Works agreements
likewise may be negotiated only by the most representative unions.

CHAPTER 5

UNION SECURITY ARRANGEMENTS

In many countries the law guarantees, either directly or indirectly, the right of an individual to refuse to adhere to a trade union organisation and forbids the exercise of any constraint which would require an individual to become a union member or supporter.[1] This right is referred to as negative freedom of association.

On the other hand, in a substantial number of countries union security arrangements, which make some form of union adherence or financial support obligatory, are permitted under the law and exist in practice to a varying degree. These arrangements may take the form of a closed shop,[2] union shop,[3] agency shop,[4] or qualified or unqualified preference.[5] Their primary functions are to strengthen the position of the union in its dealings with the employer and its control over the workforce and to ensure that all employees who reap the benefits of the union's efforts contribute a fair share thereto.

As a result of the debates which took place prior to the adoption of Convention No. 87 and especially of the rejection by the Committee on Freedom of Association of the International Labour Conference of an amendment which would have accorded to workers the "right not to join" an organisation,[6] the ILO has determined that Article 2 of the Convention "leaves it to the practice and regulations of each State to decide whether it is the right of workers ... not to join an occupational organisation, or on the other hand, to authorise and, where necessary, to regulate the use

----

[1] Such is the case, for example, in Austria, Benin, the Central African Empire, Chad, Costa Rica, the Dominican Republic, Ecuador, France, Gabon, Guinea, Ivory Coast, Madagascar, Mali, Senegal, Togo and the non-metropolitan territory of Bermuda.

[2] An arrangement whereby the employer is required to hire only employees who are union members. Retention of union membership is also a condition of continued employment.

[3] A form of union security which lets the employer hire whoever he pleases but requires all new employees to become union members within a specified period of time thereafter.

[4] An arrangement obliging all employees to pay dues or service charges to a union. Non-union employees, however, are not required to join a union as a condition of employment.

[5] A type of union security under which the employer agrees to give first preference in hiring, etc. to individuals who are union members.

[6] ILO: Record of Proceedings, International Labour Conference, 30th Session, Geneva, 1947, p. 571.

of security clauses and practice.[1] The ILO supervisory bodies
consider, however, that the position is different "when the law
imposes union security" on the workers concerned, particularly by
making union membership compulsory.[2] The ILO has compared such
provisions to those establishing a trade union monopoly which, as
was pointed out in Chapter 2 above, is not compatible with the right
of workers to establish and join the organisations of their own
choosing.

The purpose of this chapter will be to examine a variety of
provisions for union security to be found in the legislation of
various countries.

The right to enter into union security arrangements has been
recognised by the legislation of the United States since 1935.[3] In
that year the United States Congress enacted the National Labor
Relations Act, the purpose of which was to encourage the practice
and procedure of collective bargaining and to protect the right of
workers to full freedom of association. In order to achieve these
ends, the Act provided, inter alia, that it is an unfair labour
practice for an employer to discriminate against a worker in order
to encourage or discourage union membership. A proviso was attached
to the clause, however, permitting the establishment of a closed
shop; i.e. it allowed an employer to enter into a collective
bargaining agreement with a union which lawfully represented the
employees in a bargaining unit requiring, as a condition of
employment, that every employee be a member of the union. The
proviso was motivated by a desire to grant unions the stability to
maintain strong organisations insulated against fluctuations in
membership provoked by changes in the economy or labour market.

In 1947, the Labor Management Relations Act was enacted which
amended and modified the National Labor Relations Act. The new
legislation significantly altered the status of union security by
outlawing the closed shop and substituting a limited form of union
shop in its place. Under the Labor Management Relations Act, prior
union membership can no longer be made a condition for employment.
A union security arrangement is permissible, however, requiring all
employees to join the union within 30 days of either the
commencement of their employment cr the effective date of the
collective bargaining agreement. If an employee fails to comply,
the union may demand that he be dismissed by the employer.

There are two conditions under which an employer may not
dismiss an employee even though the employee has not become a union
----

[1] ILO: Report of the Committee of Experts, 1959, op. cit., p.
109, para. 36.

[2] ILO: Freedom of association and collective bargaining: General
survey, 1973, op. cit., para. 77. See also Committee on Freedom of
Association (see Appendix B, item 21).

[3] For a fuller analysis of the legality of union security
clauses in the United States, see "Union security", in Charles O.
Morris (ed.): The developing labor law (Washington, DC, Bureau of
National Affairs, 1971), pp. 697-725, plus annual supplements; and
ILO: The trade union situation in the United States: Report of a
mission from the International Labour Office (Geneva, 1960), pp. 67-
71.

member. If the employer has sufficient grounds for believing that (1) union membership was not available to the employee on the same terms and conditions generally applicable to the other members or that (2) membership was denied or revoked for reasons other than the employee's failure to tender the periodic dues and initiation fees uniformly required as a condition of acquiring or retaining union membership, he is not justified in terminating the employee. A union which exerts pressure on an employer to discriminate against an employee in violation of these legal principles or which charges an unreasonable initiation fee is guilty of an unfair labour practice.

As the law has been interpreted, a worker is in compliance with the terms of a union security agreement merely by tendering the initiation fees and periodic dues. It is not necessary for him to comply with any other conditions laid down in the union rules, such as attending union meetings or taking an oath of loyalty.[1] Thus, if an employee is not accepted by a union or is expelled on grounds other than failure to pay his dues, he is entitled to keep his job and may not be discharged by the employer.

Under the original version of the Labor Management Relations Act, a union was not permitted to seek to negotiate a union-shop agreement without obtaining the approval, by means of an authorisation election, of the majority of workers in the bargaining unit concerned. In 1951, this requirement was repealed as being unnecessary since workers had voted in favour of the union shop in 97 per cent of the elections held.[2] In its place provision is now made for a union shop de-authorisation election, pursuant to which a majority of the employees in the bargaining unit may deprive the union of the authority to continue a union security arrangement already in effect.[3]

Perhaps the Labor Management Relations Act's most controversial amendment to the National Labor Relations Act is section 14(b). This section permits States to enact legislation which outrightly prohibits "arrangements requiring membership in a labor organisation as a condition of employment". At present 20 States[4] have availed themselves of the opportunity to enact such legislation, commonly known as "right to work" laws. These States

----

[1] See, for example: Union Starch and Refining Co., 87 NLRB 779, 25 LRRM 1176 (1949); enforced, 186 F.2d 1008 (CA 7, 1951), cert. denied, 342 US 815 (1951).

[2] See Bureau of National Affairs: The developing labor law, op. cit., p. 700.

[3] A de-authorisation election must be held by the National Labor Relations Board if 30 per cent of the workers in the bargaining unit petition for the waiving of the union security clause, provided that no such election was held in the preceding 12 months.

[4] The States which have enacted right to work legislation either by statute or by constitutional amendment are as follows: Alabama, Arizona, Arkansas, Florida, Georgia, Iowa, Kansas, Louisiana (affecting agricultural workers only), Mississippi, Nebraska, Nevada, North Carolina, North Dakota, South Carolina, South Dakota, Tennessee, Texas, Utah, Virginia and Wyoming.

are primarily agricultural in character and many are located in the south. As such, they lack a deeply entrenched tradition of trade unionism and, consequently, are dominated by opponents of all systems of union security.

Alternative forms of union security less stringent than the union shop are permitted in the United States.[1] The two most frequent are the maintenance-of-membership agreement and the agency shop. Maintenance-of-membership provisions require all employees who are union members at the time of the execution of the collective bargaining agreement or at a given time thereafter, as well as all employees who later become members, to retain their union membership as a condition of continued employment. Non-union members, however, are under no duty to join the organisation. Maintenance-of-membership provisions often provide for an escape period during which time the employees may resign their union membership without being discharged. As is the case with the union shop, the membership requirement is fulfilled so long as the employee continues to pay his dues.

The agency shop has been classified by one source as "a hybrid form of union security".[2] Its purpose is, inter alia, to provide a theoretical alternative to the requirement of union membership under a union shop. Accordingly, agency-shop agreements normally provide that employees must, as a condition of continued employment, either become members of the union as under a union shop or, in the alternative, remain non-members but pay the union a service fee which usually equals the amount of the union dues. Agency-shop agreements, like their union-shop counterparts, may be prohibited by state right to work laws.[3]

The union security legislation of the United Kingdom has recently undergone a transformation. In 1971, the Government of the United Kingdom enacted the Industrial Relations Act and thereby sought to limit the use of closed-shop (known in the United Kingdom as pre-entry closed-shop) and union-shop (known as post-entry closed-shop) agreements. The legislation granted workers, as between themselves and their employers, the right to refuse to join a trade union provided that no "approved closed-shop agreement" was in force. Pre-entry closed-shop agreements were specifically outlawed and post-entry agreements were not permitted unless approved by an order of the Industrial Court. In their place the Act permitted the execution of agency-shop agreements requiring, as a condition of employment, either membership in a certain registered trade union or, in lieu of membership, the payment of "appropriate contributions". In the event that an employee objected on grounds of conscience to paying contributions to a trade union, he was permitted to pay "equivalent contributions" to a charity determined jointly by him and the trade union. A charitable contribution as an alternative to union membership was also permitted where an approved closed-shop agreement was in force.

----

[1] See, in this regard: NLRB v. General Motors Corp., 373 US 734 (1963).

[2] Bureau of National Affairs: The developing labor law, op. cit., p. 707.

[3] Local 1625, Retail Clerks International Association v. Schermerhorn, 373 US 746 (1963), on reargument, 375 US 96 (1963).

The Trade Union and Labour Relations Act, 1974, which repealed and replaced the Industrial Relations Act, undertook to alter the law regarding union security. This legislation has in turn been recently amended and further broadened by the Trade Union and Labour Relations (Amendment) Act, 1976. As presently provided, the conclusion of both pre-entry and post-entry closed-shop agreements is permitted. The legislation stipulates that the dismissal of an employee by an employer must be regarded as "fair" if "it is the practice, in accordance with a union membership agreement, for the employees for the time being of the same class as the dismissed employee to belong to a specified independent trade union, or to one of a number of specified independent trade unions; and the reason for the dismissal was that the employee was not a member of the specified union or one of the specified unions, or had refused or proposed to refuse to become or remain a member of that union or one of those unions". A "union membership agreement" is defined in the legislation as an agreement or arrangement made or existing between one or more independent trade unions and one or more employers or employers' associations which has the effect in practice of requiring the employees for the time being of the class to which it relates (whether or not there is a condition to that effect in their contract of employment) to be or become members of the union or one of the unions which is or are parties to the agreement or arrangement or of another specified independent trade union.

Under the 1974 legislation there were two circumstances in which an employee was not required to comply with a union membership agreement. These were when "the employee genuinely objects on grounds of religious belief to being a member of any trade union whatsoever or on any reasonable grounds to being a member of a particular trade union". In such cases his dismissal was deemed "unfair" and was therefore actionable. The amending Act of 1976 has, however, repealed the exemption of an employee who objects "on any reasonable grounds to being a member of a particular trade union". Thus, under the present legislation the dismissal of an employee for violation of a union membership agreement is regarded as "unfair" only if he can show that he objects to joining any union on grounds of religious belief.

The legislation of the Philippines, like that of the United States, permits union security by creating an exception to the general provision relating to unfair labour practices of employers. The provision prohibits an employer from discriminating "in regard to wages, hours of work and other terms and conditions of employment in order to encourage or discourage membership in any labor organization". However, no unfair labour practice is committed if an employer and the union serving as the collective bargaining agent enter into an agreement requiring membership in the union as a condition for employment. Such an agreement may not apply to employees who are already members of another union at the time of the signing of the collective bargaining agreement. The union, in turn, is guilty of an unfair labour practice if it causes or attempts to cause an employer to discriminate against an employee who has been denied union membership or to terminate an employee "on any ground other than the usual terms and conditions under which membership is made available to other members".

The Philippine legislation also authorises the establishment of an agency shop. The law stipulates that employees in an appropriate collective bargaining unit who are not members of the recognised collective bargaining agent may be assessed a "reasonable fee equivalent to the dues and other fees paid by members of the recognised collective bargaining agent". Non-union members who do not pay such a fee may be denied the benefits accorded under the collective bargaining agreement.

In Japan the establishment of a closed shop is permitted by law. The Japanese legislation provides that an employer may conclude a trade agreement with a trade union requiring, as a condition of employment, that the workers be members of the trade union if such trade union represents a majority of the workers in a particular plant or workplace.

The execution of a closed-shop agreement is also authorised in Mexico, where legislation permits an employer to agree to employ only those individuals who are already members of the contracting union and to discharge those who resign or are expelled from it. Such an agreement may not be applied so as to prejudice non-members of the union already employed in the undertaking prior to the date of the conclusion of the agreement.

In Australia[1] and New Zealand, where the industrial relations systems are based upon compulsory arbitration, qualified and unqualified (or absolute) preference provisions constitute, as a general rule, the permitted forms of union security. Such provisions may be either negotiated by the parties or inserted into a collective agreement by the applicable industrial relations commission (the Commonwealth Conciliation and Arbitration Commission in the case of Australia and the Industrial Commission in the case of New Zealand).

The legislation of New Zealand defines a qualified preference provision as "a provision to the effect that if any employer bound by the award or agreement engages or employs, in any position or employment that is subject to the award or agreement, any adult person (other than a person who holds a current certificate of exemption from union membership ...) who is not a member of a union of workers bound by the award or agreement and who fails to become a member of such a union within 14 days after his engagement, or, as the case may require, after the provision comes into force, or who fails to remain a member of the union so long as he continues in the position or employment, the employer shall cease to employ that person when requested to do so by any officer or authorised representative of the union, provided that - (i) such person has, at any time since his engagement, been requested to become a member of the union ...; and (ii) there is a member of the union equally qualified to perform the particular work required to be done and ready and willing to undertake it ...".

The definition of an unqualified preference provision, on the other hand, is like that of a union shop;[2] it contains no provisos and requires a non-exempt employee, as a condition of employment and

----

[1] While most of the States of Australia have enacted their own legislation dealing with union security, this study will concern itself only with the federal, or Commonwealth, system.

[2] This is, in fact, the predominant form of union security in New Zealand.

upon penalty of discharge, to become and remain a member of the union regardless of whether or not their exists an equally qualified union member available to assume the job in question.

While the legislation contains no requirements limiting the application of a qualified preference provision, an unqualified preference may not be awarded, or an agreement containing such a provision may not be registered, unless 50 per cent or more of the workers concerned desire to become or remain members of the union which is a party to the agreement. In order to demonstrate the necessary support, the union may apply to the Registrar of Industrial Unions for the holding of a secret ballot.

Every worker "who is not of general bad character" is granted the right to union membership by the legislation. However, a union whose "maximum membership is fixed by or in accordance with any Act or award or collective agreement or order of the Commission" is not obliged to admit an individual if his admission would require the union to exceed its prescribed maximum membership. An employee is entitled to be exempted from the requirement of union membership if he can show that he objects to becoming or remaining a member of the union on the grounds of conscientious belief. "Conscientious belief" is defined in the legislation as "any conscientious belief honestly, sincerely, and personally held, whether or not the grounds of the belief are of a religious character, and whether or not the belief is part of the doctrine of any religion, religious denomination, or sect". An exempted employee is required to pay the amount of the applicable union dues and fees to the Government's Consolidated Revenue Account or, in the alternative, to the union concerned to be applied by it to any union welfare fund or to a charitable purpose.

In Australia, the Commonwealth Conciliation and Arbitration Commission may direct that union preference in employment shall be given where, in its opinion, "it is necessary for the prevention or settlement of an industrial dispute, for ensuring that effect will be given to the purposes and objectives of an award, for the maintenance of industrial peace or for the welfare of society". Although the legislation does not so specify, the preference granted by the Commission or negotiated by the parties may be either absolute or qualified.[1] The definitions and interpretation accorded to these two terms in Australia differ slightly from those accorded to their New Zealand counterparts. Under an absolute preference provision, an employer is compelled to give unconditional priority to a union member and may only employ a non-unionist if no union member is available. Under qualified preference, a union member must be employed ahead of a non-union member provided "other things are equal"; i.e. that the union member is at least as competent and qualified as the non-unionist. The granting of preference, whether absolute or qualified, applies primarily to the employment of new

----

[1] See, in this regard: The King v. Wallis, 786 CLR 529 and The King v. Findlay, 81 CLR 531 (1950). See also Kenneth F. Walker: Australian Industrial Relations Systems (Cambridge, Mass., Harvard University Press, 1970), pp. 3-43; and R.M. Martin, "Legal enforcement of union security in Australia", in J.E. Isaac and G.W. Ford (eds.): Australian labour relations - Readings (Melbourne, Sun Books, 2nd ed., 1971), pp. 166-191.

labour but may be extended to cover promotions and retrenchment.[1]
The Commonwealth Conciliation and Arbitration Commission is not
authorised to award or order compulsory unionism such as a closed
shop; however, it may certify an agreement providing for compulsory
unionism if it is voluntarily agreed upon by the parties.[2]

As in New Zealand, a person whose conscientious beliefs do not
permit him to be a member of a labour organisation may be exempted
from the coverage of a preference provision.[3] The legislation of
Australia empowers the Industrial Registrar to issue exemption
certificates. While a certificate is in force, an employer is not
bound to give preference in hiring to union members over the
certificate's holder. In order to obtain and/or renew an exemption
certificate, an individual must convince the Registrar of his
conscientious belief and pay to the Government an amount equal to
the dues and fees paid by his fellow workers who are union members.

In Trinidad and Tobago the establishment of an agency shop may
be ordered by the Registration Recognition and Certification Board,
a body empowered to deal with industrial relations questions. A
recognised majority union may at any time apply to the Board for an
agency-shop order. In considering whether to entertain the
application, the Board must have regard to, in particular, "the
constitution of the union", "the admission, subscription and other
dues or levies authorised by the rules of the union" and "the
circumstances in which a person may join the union and resign from
it". It must also be "satisfied that the holders of offices in the
union are elected and removable by simple majority in a democratic
manner and that any power to waive the payment of dues ... is
limited to cases of genuine hardship and in accordance with good
industrial relations practice".

If the Board is satisfied that it is proper to make an agency-
shop order, it must first make a provisional order for the purpose.
Within 28 days of the making of a provisional order the Board must
take an agency-shop ballot among the workers in the bargaining unit.
If two-thirds or more of the workers vote in favour of the agency
shop, the provisional order is made final and enters into force;
otherwise, the provisional order is cancelled and the union
concerned may not apply again for an agency-shop order until at
least two years have elapsed since its last application.

Under a final agency-shop order, the employer is required to
deduct from every employee the amount of the union contribution.[4]
This amount is determined by the Board but presumably equals the

----

[1] See Walker, op. cit., p. 37.

[2] See Martin, loc. cit., p. 176.

[3] The legislation defines "conscientious beliefs" as "any
conscientious beliefs whether the grounds for the beliefs are or are
not of a religious character and whether the beliefs are or are not
part of the doctrine of any religion".

[4] The contribution is apparently deducted from union and non-
union members alike and thus replaces any other method previously
used by the union to collect its dues and fees.

amount of the dues and fees set by the union. If an employee so authorises, the employer is required to turn over to the union the whole of the union contribution. In the absence of such an authorisation the union receives 50 per cent of the contribution. The remaining 50 per cent is turned over to a Labour College established under an Act of 1972 or, if the employee prefers, to the Industrial Relations Charitable Fund "for the use of institutions or organisations for the physically and mentally handicapped".

In Switzerland[1] a form of union security similar to the agency shop is permitted and practised. Although compulsory unionism is outlawed, collective agreements may nevertheless require contributions of solidarity to be paid by all non-union employees. As is the case with an agency shop, the system of contributions of solidarity requires every worker covered by and benefiting from a collective agreement to pay his share of the costs of collective bargaining without being compelled to belong to the contracting union. Under the Swiss formulation the contributions usually equal approximately 90 per cent of the union dues. They are not permitted to be excessive and the Swiss courts are authorised to decide in each case whether the agreed upon contribution is reasonable. The contributions may be used only to defray the costs involved in the execution and application of the collective agreement or for welfare purposes which benefit all the employees - union and non-union members alike - in the bargaining unit. In addition, a member of a union which is not a party to the collective agreement may not be compelled to pay a contribution of solidarity unless his union is granted an opportunity to join the original agreement or to sign a similar one.

The legislation of Sweden does not specifically mention union security; nevertheless, it sets the limits within which such agreements may freely operate. The legislation deals with freedom of association and guarantees all workers "the right to belong to an association, to exercise their rights as members of the association, and to work for the association or for the formation of an association".[2] It further provides that "the right of association shall be deemed to be infringed" if measures are taken either by employers or by employees which (1) constrain an employee or (2) are calculated to cause prejudice to an employee in the exercise of his guaranteed rights, "even if the measures in question have been taken under a clause of a collective contract or any other contract".

As this legislation has been interpreted by the Labour Court,[3] union security provisions, including closed-shop clauses, are not
----

[1] For a fuller discussion of the Swiss system of union security, see Alexandre Berenstein: "Union security and the scope of collective agreements in Switzerland", in International Labour Review (Geneva, ILO), Feb. 1962, pp. 101-121; and M. Dudra: "The Swiss system of union security", in Labor Law Journal (Chicago, Commerce Clearing House), Mar. 1959, pp. 165-174.

[2] The right of negative freedom of association is not guaranteed by the legislation, however.

[3] See ILO: The trade union situation in Sweden: Report of a mission from the International Labour Office (Geneva, 1961), pp. 29-32; see also Committee on Freedom of Association (Appendix B, item 56).

regarded as infringing the right of association, whilst the agreements themselves are legally binding and enforceable. On the other hand, a union security agreement may not prevent a worker from choosing the union to which he wants to belong. Thus, an employer may enter into an agreement requiring membership in a union as a condition of employment;[1] however, he will be in violation of the legislation if he dismisses or threatens to dismiss an employee who is already a member of another union for refusing to join the union with which the agreement was concluded.[2] If an employee is wrongfully dismissed he may be reinstated by the Labour Court.

None of the countries whose legislation has now been examined makes union security compulsory, nor do any of them single out a particular trade union to be the beneficiary of a union security arrangement. Such is not the case, however, in a few countries, including the Congo and Tanzania. The legislation of the Congo requires all employers to deduct a monthly contribution from the wages of every employee. The contribution, which is set at 0.50 per cent of a worker's monthly salary, goes to the benefit of the Congolese Trade Union Confederation.

In Tanzania the Minister of Labour is empowered to impose a union shop wherever the number of members of the National Union of Tanganyika Workers constitutes 50 per cent or more of the total number of persons employed in the enterprise or undertaking. Under the provisions of the union shop, all employees must become union members within two months either of the commencement of their employment or of the entry into force of the union shop order and must thereafter retain their union membership.[3] An employer is required, subject to penalty, to discharge any employee who fails to comply with the order notwithstanding "any agreement for notice ... or the provisions of any other law relating to notice", or provision of law. Moreover, no severance allowance is payable to the employee whose employment is terminated.

----

[1] The rules of the Swedish Employers' Confederation (SAF) provide that collective agreements concluded by a member of SAF and a trade union must contain a clause stipulating the right of the employer to avail himself of workers belonging to any organisation whatsoever, or to none.

[2] The employer may require a job applicant to be a member of a particular union as a condition of prior employment in the case of a closed-shop clause, however.

[3] Union-shop provisions do not apply, however, to "any person who is, by any other written law, prohibited from or declared ineligible for becoming a member of a trade union; or any person in receipt of a salary not less than 14,040 shillings per annum who performs managerial functions".

CONCLUSIONS

The principle, as set forth in Convention No. 87, that workers have the right to establish and join the organisations of their own choosing is generally accepted as one of the foundations of freedom of association. Implicit in the explicitly stated right are a right to decide the structure and composition of unions, a right to set up one or more organisations for a given undertaking, trade or industry and a right to establish federations and confederations in each case without governmental interference. The present study has examined the legislation of many countries bearing on these rights and has shown that their exercise often gives rise to difficulties. Outstanding among these is the problem of harmonising free trade union choice with the development of a united and powerful trade union movement.

It is commonly accepted that society derives benefits from an orderly, well-organised and independent trade union structure and that such a structure is rarely achieved with a multiplicity of small and competing labour organisations. There is, consequently, an understandable desire on the part of many governments to foster the development of large and effective trade unions. Governments seeking to encourage workers to form strong and effective organisations should keep in mind, however, that restrictions imposed by legislation whereby workers are denied the free choice of the union to which they may wish to belong run counter to the principles of freedom of association.

Accordingly, in examining the legislation and actions of the member countries in relation to the principle of free trade union choice, the ILO supervisory bodies distinguish between the beneficial encouragement of trade union strength and the unilateral imposition of trade union unity. In drawing that distinction, the Committee of Experts on the Application of Conventions and Recommendations and the Committee on Freedom of Association consider that trade union monopoly, imposed by legislative means, raises one of the most difficult problems of conformity with the principle of freedom of association. As an alternative to such systems, as well as to deal with the question of trade union recognition for purposes of collective bargaining, the supervisory bodies favourably consider legislation providing for the selection of the most representative trade union. Such legislation grants special rights, particularly with regard to collective bargaining, to the union which represents the majority or a certain proportion of the workers concerned, and is considered to be in conformity with the Freedom of Association and Protection of the Right to Organise Convention (No. 87) provided that basic objective criteria for the prevention of unfair discrimination among unions are applied.

Both the Committee of Experts and the Committee on Freedom of Association have also been concerned with other aspects of free trade union choice. They consider that legislation which creates unreasonable minimum membership or regional requirements or which unduly limits the right of public servants, agricultural workers or managerial staff to establish and join the unions of their choice or which restricts the creation of federations and confederations or which involves racial discrimination is not compatible with the guarantees set forth in Convention No. 87.

On the other hand, actions taken by governments to foster, on a voluntary basis, the establishment of coherent and well-organised trade union movements do not run counter to the principles of the Convention. Reasonable minimum membership provisions may not be incompatible with the Convention. Requirements that primary organisations be established on an occupational or industrial basis are deemed to be purely formal in nature so long as such organisations have the right to establish inter-occupational or inter-industrial federations and confederations. Similarly, governments are not obliged to permit the establishment of joint public and private sector primary labour organisations, and genuine managerial and supervisory staff, whose interests may conflict with those of the workers whom they supervise, may be restricted to organisations of like personnel. Furthermore, systems of union security, such as the closed shop, union shop, agency shop or preference agreements have been deliberately excluded from the province of the Freedom of Association Convention. It is accordingly left to the practice and regulations of each country to decide whether it is appropriate to guarantee the right not to join an organisation or to authorise and regulate the use of union security clauses.

Thus acceptance of the right of workers to establish and join the organisations of their own choosing need not result in a weak and disorganised trade union movement. As shown in this study, governments have at their option many substantial and effective means of developing trade union coherence and strength without violating the principle of freedom of association. It is, however, with the trade unions themselves that the main responsibilities lie for organising themselves in a way that will best defend and promote the interests of their members.

Appendix A: Some case studies of discrimination by public authorities

The right of workers to establish and join the organisations of their own choosing may be affected not only by the applicable labour legislation but also by the attitude adopted and displayed by public authorities. Such authorities, by their very nature, have the power to influence and coerce; those who do use it either to favour one union or to discriminate against another may seriously impair the right of free trade union choice.

In some countries trade union legislation may foster the adoption of discriminatory attitudes by granting certain public authorities great discretion in the performance of their duties. In other cases, however, the authorities may attempt to interfere with the establishment or continued existence of a labour organisation without any legislative support. Whatever the case, however, the principle of freedom of association requires that the right of workers to establish and join the organisations of their own choosing must be guaranteed in fact as well as by law.[1] Thus, it is not enough that the relevant legislation permits free trade union choice; what is also necessary is that the attitude adopted by public authorities shall not hinder the exercise of the right to that choice. Some of the cases analysed and adjudicated by the Committee on Freedom of Association will be considered below for the purpose of pointing to several methods of interference with the free establishment and maintenance of trade unions that have sometimes been used by public authorities.

A first form of interference concerns the registration of trade unions and the granting of legal personality. As was noted in Chapter 2 above, there are many countries where a trade union cannot come into lawful existence or effectively represent its members unless it has been registered. In most cases, trade unions will be registered if they satisfy all the technical requirements prescribed in the legislation, such as filing copies of the union rules and a list of the elected officers with the trade union Registrar. Occasionally, however, the public authorities exercise their power to refuse either lawfully or unlawfully, registration, in order to prevent or delay the establishment of a union towards which they are not favourably disposed.

In one case,[2] the complainant trade union alleged that the Ministry of Labour had failed to legalise and register it although

----

[1] See, for example, Committee on Freedom of Association (Appendix B, item 1), in which the following statement is made: "The Committee notes that the provisions in the Constitution and the Labour Code ... [of the country in question] at present in force with respect to the right of association and other fundamental liberties appear to be satisfactory. At the same time, the Committee wishes to emphasise the importance that it attaches to the fact that workers and employers should in actual practice be able to form and join the organisations of their own choosing in full freedom."

[2] Committee on Freedom of Association (see Appendix B, item 45; for a similar case, see item 62).

it had complied with all the conditions prescribed in the legislation. The legislation required the administrative authorities either to register the applicant union or to make whatever observations it deemed pertinent within two months of the receipt of all the appropriate documents. In this case, however, the authorities took no action until 14 months had elapsed from the date of the request for registration. Moreover, they gave no explanation for the delay. In determining that their failure to act was in contravention of the right to organise, the Committee on Freedom of Association stated as follows: "As regards the considerable delay in the Ministry's decision as compared with the time limit allowed under national law, the Committee has stated on more than one occasion that the purpose of the whole procedure for the examination of cases where a violation of freedom of association is alleged is to promote respect for trade union rights, both de jure and de facto, and that the workers' right freely to constitute organisations of their own choice cannot be considered to exist until such time as it is fully recognised and observed both de facto and de jure."[1]

In another case,[2] not dissimilar from the first, the authorities also ignored the registration provisions of the labour legislation. The complainants alleged that a union had been set up in an undertaking comprising practically all its workers and had submitted to the authorities the necessary documentation for registration. The authorities had, however, refused to register the union because the undertaking had concluded a collective agreement with another trade union. The complainants maintained that the authorities had violated a legislative provision prohibiting refusal to register an organisation which had complied with the formal requirements. The union had instituted an appeal before a competent court, which found that, as the law permitted the existence of more than one trade union in one and the same undertaking and prohibited refusal of registration if all the basic and formal requirements laid down by the law had been complied with, the existence of a collective agreement with another union in the same undertaking did not constitute an obstacle to registration.

In yet another case, a union of public servants was denied registration.[3] Although the country's legislation entitled employees of the official services to establish trade unions, the government authorities stated that the employees concerned were not entitled to the legislation's protection because, since there was no regular civil service in the country, they were only de facto employees of the State who did not yet enjoy de jure guarantees. Pointing out that the workers' right freely to constitute organisations of their own choice must be "fully recognised and observed both de facto and de jure", the Committee on Freedom of Association found as follows: "The present case relates to public officials who established a trade union and applied for it to be registered and granted legal personality with a view to normal operation within the framework of the law. However, although there were no major formal obstacles to registration, according to the outline of events submitted to the

----

[1] ibid. (see Appendix 3, item 44).

[2] ibid. (see Appendix B, item 35; see also item 50).

[3] ibid. (see Appendix B, items 37 and 47).

Committee, the authorities did not register the union, nor did they consequently grant it legal personality without which the organisation cannot lawfully exist. In these circumstances the Committee must expressly emphasise, as it has on other occasions, the importance of ensuring that persons employed in the service of the State should be guaranteed the right to establish trade unions and to register them with a view to their lawful operation."[1]

In the above cases the public authorities disregarded the applicable legislation in order to deny registration to qualified trade unions. In other instances, however, the legislation grants the authorities such broad discretion that they may discriminate against labour organisations within the framework of the law. There have been cases, for example, where the legislation has empowered the authorities to refuse registration or to dissolve an already registered union if, in their opinion, a trade union was contrary to public order or "likely to be used for unlawful purposes or purposes inconsistent with its objects or rules", or would "not be able to implement any of the provisions contained in its rules".[2]

Two such cases have been considered by the Committee on Freedom of Association. In one of them,[3] the law empowered the authorities to refuse final registration of a trade union if they considered that it had not yet attained "a reasonable degree of efficiency and organisation in the management of its affairs", but allowed an appeal from such a decision. Commenting on that legislation, the Committee stated as follows: "The Committee considers that the provision ... [in question] gives excessive scope to the ... [authorities concerned] in determining whether registration should or should not be granted to an industrial association. Even though the law permits an appeal ... from the ... decision, the Committee recalls that in such cases the Committee of Experts on the Application of Conventions and Recommendations has pointed out that 'the existence of a procedure of appeal to the courts does not appear to be a sufficient guarantee; in effect, this does not alter the nature of the powers conferred on the authorities responsible for effecting registration, and the judges hearing such an appeal ... would only be able to ensure that the legislation had been correctly applied'. The Committee accordingly considers ... that the law should contain a clear definition of the specific conditions to be satisfied by trade unions in order to qualify for registration and that specific statutory criteria should be prescribed for the purposes of deciding whether these conditions have been satisfied."[4]

In the second case, the legislation freely permitted formal registration but authorised the authorities concerned "to raise an objection to the setting up of a trade union within a period of three months from the date of registration of its by-laws". A union

----

[1] ibid. (see Appendix B, item 37).

[2] See, ILO: Freedom of association and collective bargaining: General survey, op. cit., para. 59.

[3] Committee on Freedom of Association (see Appendix B, items 36 and 42).

[4] ibid. (see Appendix B, item 36).

to whose establishment an objection had been raised was notified
that it must "refrain from engaging in any trade union activities".[1]
In the view of the Committee on Freedom of Association, "a
legislative provision of this kind is in direct contradiction with
the basic principle according to which employers and workers should
have the right to establish organisations of their choice without
prior authorisation".[2]

A second form of interference consists in the dissemination by
public authorities by means of speeches, press releases or
proclamations, of prejudicial anti-union information, such as
warnings against union membership, threats to dissolve the union or
disparagement of the union's reputation. Cases involving anti-union
information are particularly difficult to analyse because they
require the striking of a delicate balance between freedom of
association and freedom of speech. The Committee on Freedom of
Association has stated its view of such cases as follow: "The
question at issue is connected with the problem of free speech and
its limits. The Committee has already had occasion to point out
that 'the right to express opinions through the press or otherwise
is clearly one of the essential elements of trade union rights'.
While freedom of expression must therefore be accorded to trade
union organisations, it is evident that the same freedom cannot be
denied to governments. In other words, for example, if a government
has been the subject of attack or criticism by trade unions, it
would be normal for it to have the right to reply and to make known
its point of view and for such reply to receive the same publicity
as did the attacks made on the government. The government should
not, however, exercise such freedom of expression in such terms and
by such means - in particular, by utilisation of the machinery of
the State - as to assume a coercive character and infringe the right
of workers to belong to organisations of their own choosing."[3]

Because of the need to weigh a government's right of
expression, the Committee has formulated the following standard for
evaluating cases of anti-union propaganda: "... the question as to
how far the attitude publicly adopted by a government towards a
trade union organisation constitutes an infringement of the workers'
right to belong to organisations of their own choosing would seem to
depend essentially on factual circumstances; it might depend, for
example, on the terms in which the government complained against
expressed its point of view, on the conditions in which this view
was brought to the notice of the public or of the workers concerned
(press, utilisation of the machinery of the State, etc.) and on any
other elements which might make it possible to judge whether the

----

[1] ibid. (see Appendix B, item 13).

[2] ibid. (see Appendix B, item 14).

[3] Committee on Freedom of Association (see Appendix B, item 4).
This case involved an allegation by the complainant union that
government authorities had prepared and distributed pamphlets among
the workers in the trade concerned which warned them not to trust
the union and slandered the organisation in violent terms. The
Committee's finding being, however, that the union had adduced no
conclusive proof in support of its contention, it recommended the
Governing Body of the ILO "to decide that the case does not call for
further examination".

position taken up by the government did or did not assume a coercive character or might probably have exercised pressure on the workers concerned."[1]

In another case[2] involving anti-union information, the complainant union alleged that, in an official publication, pressure had been exercised on the employees of a government department not to join trade unions. Referring to those organisations as "illegal so-called unions" and as "unscrupulous people", the publication declared that "they cannot assist you in any of your service conditions; yes, they are only out to collect your money. They are living off the fat of the land, and that with your hard earned money which you contribute to them monthly. As a matter of fact, activities related to these unions, of whatever nature they may be, are not permitted on ... [the] premises [in question]."[3] The Committee on Freedom of Association found that it was clear from the publication that the authorities had exercised presure on workers "to induce them not to join trade unions" and that it constituted an infringement of the principle that workers "without distinction whatsoever" should have "the right to establish and ... to join the organisations of their own choosing without previous authorisation".

In another case,[4] the Minister of the Interior made a statement to his country's press agency to the effect "that the Government intended to dissolve" a federation of trade unions. As the threat was never put into effect, the Committee on Freedom of Association accordingly drew attention "to the danger of statements of that kind being interpreted as meaning that the Government had in fact decided to enforce such a dissolution of a central trade union organisation of workers" and "as intended to exert pressure on workers when exercising their right to join organisations of their own choosing".

The complainant union in a further case[5] alleged that "all the government machinery" had been directed towards forcing workers, by the use of threats, to withdraw from a union and to join another union. According to the complainant, the authorities sought to destroy the union "because the continual agitation of that trade union organisation was detrimental to the Government's interests since the increases in wages and welfare benefits were reducing the tax receipts from the ... industry [in question]. Such receipts were necessary to the Government, which would break down without them".[6] The Government, however, categorically denied that it participated in the campaign. Although the basic conflict of evidence made it impossible for the Committee on Freedom of Association to ascertain the true factual position, it nevertheless drew attention to the principle that workers should have the right

----

[1] ibid. (see Appendix B, item 5).

[2] ibid. (see Appendix B, item 39).

[3] ibid. (see Appendix B, item 40).

[4] ibid. (see Appendix B, item 46).

[5] ibid. (see Appendix B, item 29).

[6] ibid. (see Appendix B, item 30).

to establish and join trade unions of their own choosing and it
expressed the hope that all necessary and appropriate measures would
be taken to ensure that the workers "may freely exercise the right
to organise".

Anti-union information was combined with discriminatory
legislative action to hinder a trade union organisational drive in
another case.[1] The complainant alleged that a government leader had
"launched a campaign of abuse against the union and tried to deprive
it of the collective bargaining rights it had secured by scrupulous
adherence to the legal processes, calling on the ... [employees
concerned] to leave the union and join a union which the Government
would sponsor". In addition, a resolution condemning the union had
been introduced in the legislature, as well as two laws, one of
which provided for the decertification of the union, while the other
provided for "the dissolution of certain unions and the confiscation
of their funds where 'it appears' that certain circumstances
obtain". Following upon a prolonged examination of this case and
representations to the authorities concerned, the Committee on
Freedom of Association was able to report to the Governing Body of
the ILO that legislative provisions contravening Convention No. 87
had been repealed.

Interference by public authorities has sometimes taken the
form of unequal distribution of financial aid or subsidies. In some
countries the government lends support to labour organisations
through direct grants of monetary assistance or by providing them
with headquarters, meeting halls or labour exchanges either free or
at minimal cost. If the distribution of these benefits favours one
union or is to the disadvantage of another, the workers' right to
free trade union choice may be impaired.

In one case[2] analysed by the Committee on Freedom of
Association, the country's trade union movement was divided between
two trade union federations. The complainant and more recently
formed federation alleged that its share of the government subsidies
was far smaller than that of the other federation and that sometimes
it had received no subsidies at all. It further alleged that labour
exchanges and other premises were placed at the free disposition of
the favoured federation alone, whereas it was itself compelled to
rent premises. The Government, while emphasising that it was not
seeking to favour one trade union at the expense of another, and did
not permit infringements against the right to organise, explained
that one of the federations had been in existence years before the
other and that subsidies were determined and approved primarily by
local communities, not by the national government. It also stated
that it was continually endeavouring to redress the situation caused
by these circumstances.

While noting the declaration of the Government "that it is
doing everything possible to ensure that trade unions of various
tendencies are treated with strict impartiality as regards material
benefits", the Committee also observed as follows: "When examining
former cases that showed certain similar characteristics to those of
----

[1] ibid. (see Appendix B, items 9, 12, 16, 20 and 27).

[2] ibid. (see Appendix B, item 31; for similar cases see items 17
and 51).

the present case the Committee pointed out, on the one hand, that the repercussions which financial aid may have on the autonomy of trade union organisations will depend essentially on circumstances: they cannot be assessed by applying general principles; and, on the other hand, that the fact that a government granted benefits to a certain organisation or withdrew them from it in favour of another was likely to result, even if inadvertently, in aiding or in impeding one trade union in comparison with the others and consequently to become a discriminatory action. More specifically, the Committee believed that a government, by aiding or impeding one organisation in comparison with the others, is able to influence - directly or indirectly - the choice of the workers as regards which organisation they wish to join; for it is a fact that they will be inclined to join the trade union most useful to them even if, for vocational or other reasons, they would have preferred to affiliate to some other organisation."[1]

----

[1] ibid. (see Appendix B, item 32).

Appendix B: List of references to reports of the
Committee on Freedom of Association of the
Governing Body of the ILO

In the footnotes to the study, reference to reports of the
Committee on Freedom of Associaticn are abbreviated as follows:
Committee on Freedom of Association (see Appendix B, item ...). The
following key to the item numbers gives for each item: the number of
the Committee report, the number of the case examined by the
Committee, the number of the relevant paragraph of the report and
the issue of the ILO's Official Bulletin in which the report has
been published.

Item no. in foot-notes to the study	No. of Committee report	No. of the case	No. of paragraph in report	Issue of ILO Official Bulletin
1	6	3	1024	1
2	6	55	919	1
3	15	102	141	1955, No. 1, p. 28
4	27	166	79	1958, No. 3, p. 115
5	27	166	81	1958, No. 3, p. 116
6	32	179	16	1960, No. 3, p. 144
7	36	190	203	1960, No. 3, p. 209
8	44	200	166-175	1960, No. 3, pp. 291-299
9	45	211	82-110	1960, No. 3, pp. 314-321
10	47	194	111	1961, No. 3, p. 104
11	48	191	72	1961, No. 3, p. 129
12	49	211	197-253	1961, No. 3, pp. 170-183
13	53	232	53-54	1961, No. 3, p. 270
14	53	232	55	1961, No. 3, p. 270
15	54	179	156	1961, No. 3, p. 303
16	56	211	141-145	1961, Nc. 3, pp. 334-337
17	57	248	20-59	1961, No. 3, pp. 350-356
18	58	220	38	1962, No. 1, suppl., p. 6
19	58	251	611	1962, No. 1, suppl., p. 103
20	60	211	38-74	1962, No. 2, suppl. I, pp. 18-19
21	65	266	60	1962, No. 3, suppl. II, p. 64
22	65	266	61	1962, No. 3, suppl. II, p. 64
23	66	179	351	1963, No. 1, suppl. p. 61
24	67	303	264	1963, No. 2, suppl. I, p. 40
25	67	303	292	1963, No. 2, suppl. I, p. 45
26	68	313	56	1963, No. 2, suppl. I, p. 64
27	72	211	17-28	1964, No. 1, suppl., pp. 6-8
28	74	363	230	1964, No. 3, suppl. II, p. 73
29	77	366	49-59	1964, No. 3, suppl. II, pp. 174-177
30	77	366	53	1964, No. 3, suppl. II, pp. 175-176
31	79	361	86-100	1965, No. 2, suppl. pp. 14-16
32	79	361	98	1965, No. 2, suppl., pp. 15-16
33	79	393	145	1965, No. 2, suppl., p. 29
34	83	393	63	1965, No. 3, suppl. II, pp. 25-26
35	84	394	13-22	1965, No. 3, suppl. II, pp. 92-94
36	84	415	41-62 (58,59)	1965, No. 3, suppl. II, pp. 98-103
37	84	423	68-78 (73)	1965, No. 3, suppl. II, pp. 103-107

Item no. in foot- notes to the study	No. of Committee report	No. of the case	No. of paragraph in report	Issue of ILO Official Bulletin
38	84	423	73	1965, No. 3, suppl. II, p. 105
39	85	(300) (311) (321)	59-166	1966, No. 1, suppl., pp. 12-33
40	85	(300) (311) (321)	141, 142,145, 146	1966, No. 1, suppl., p. 27
41	85	335	455	1966, No. 1, suppl., pp. 86-87
42	85	415	231-246	1966, No. 1, suppl., pp. 44-47
43	92	376	31	1966, No. 3, suppl. II, p. 85
44	92	439	162	1966, No. 3, suppl. II, p. 102
45	92	439	154-167	1966, No. 3, suppl. II, pp. 101-103
46	93	494	328-348 (333,335)	1967, No. 1, suppl., pp. 58-61
47	95	423	100-111	1967, No. 2, suppl., pp. 27-29
48	95	448	124	1967, No. 2, suppl., p. 31
49	98	503	259	1967, No. 3, suppl. II, pp. 64-65
50	101	460	59-79	1968, No. 1, suppl., pp. 10-12
51	104	522	32-48	1968, No. 4, suppl., pp. 6-8
52	105	531	283	1968, No. 4, suppl., p. 58
53	108	506	223	1969, No. 1, suppl., p. 56
54	108	506	225	1969, No. 1, suppl., p. 56
55	108	506	226	1969, No. 1, suppl., p. 57
56	119	621	25,26,32	1970, No. 4, suppl., pp. 54,55
57	120	604	150	1971, No. 2, suppl., p. 27
58	121	624	56	1971, No. 2, suppl., p. 49
59	127	660	271	1972, suppl., p. 48
60	127	660	272	1972, suppl., p. 48
61	128	662	40	1972, suppl., p. 60
62	128	675	16-21	1972, suppl., p. 57
63	135	677	155	1973, suppl., p. 40
64	138	631	30	1973, suppl., pp. 101-102

[1] See Seventh report of the International Labour Organisation to the United Nations (1953), Appendix V.

Appendix C: List of laws and regulations

The laws and regulations listed below contain the provisions
which have been examined in this study and which concern the right
of workers to establish and to join the organisations of their own
choosing.   The   list   gives   the English titles, or English
translations of the titles, of the selected laws and regulations.
The titles are given in full except where the text of a law provides
for the use of a short title. For convenience of reference, the
list also shows the numbers of the particular sections of the laws
and regulations in which the provisions described in the study may
be found.

ALGERIA

Ordinance No. 71-75, 1971 (section 2)

Ordinance No. 75-31, 1975 (section 85)

Decree No. 75-64, 1975

ARGENTINA

Act No. 20615 of 29 November 1973 respecting workers' occupational
    associations (sections 3, 19-30)

AUSTRALIA

Conciliation and Arbitration Act, 1904-1975 (sections 31, 47, 132)

BELGIUM

Collective Agreements and Joint Committees Acts, 1968 (sections 1,
    3, 5, 42)

BENIN

Labour Code, 1967 (section 5)

BOLIVIA

Labour Code, 1939 (section 103)

Presidential Decree No. 7822, 1966 (section 11)

BRAZIL

Legislative Decree   No. 5452 of 1 May 1943 to approve the
    Consolidation of Labour Laws, as amended (sections 534, 535)

BRITISH SOLOMON ISLANDS

Trade Unions Ordinance, 1966, as amended (section 2)

UNITED REPUBLIC OF CAMEROON

Order No. 24/MTLS/Decree, 1969 (sections 2, 4)

CANADA

Labour Code, 1966-1967 (sections 113-116)

CANADA: British Columbia

Human Rights Code, 1973 (section 9)

CANADA: Manitoba

Human Rights Act, 1974 (section 6)

CANADA: New Brunswick

Human Rights Act (section 3)

CANADA: Ontario

Labour Relations Act, 1960 (section 10)

CANADA: Prince Edward Island

Human Rights Code, 1968 (section 6)

CANADA: Quebec

Employment Discrimination Act, 1964 (section 3)

CANADA: Saskatchewan

Fair Employment Practice Act, 1965 (section 5)

CENTRAL AFRICAN EMPIRE

Labour Code, 1961 (section 6)

CHAD

Act No. 7-66 of 4 March 1966 to establish a Labour and Social
    Welfare Code (section 37)

COLOMBIA

Decree No. 2663 of 5 August 1950 to promulgate the Labour Code, as amended by Decree No. 3743 of 20 December 1950 (sections 373, 376)

Legislative Decree No. 2351, 1965 (section 26)

Decree No. 1373, 1966 (section 11)

CONGO

Decree No. 73-167/NJT, 1973 (sections 1, 2)

Act No. 45/75 of 15 March 1975 instituting a Labour Code (section 185)

COSTA RICA

Labour Code, 1943, as amended (sections 56, 273)

CUBA

Act No. 962 of 1 August 1961 respecting industrial associations (sections 11, 12)

CYPRUS

Public Service Act, 1969 (section 59)

CZECHOSLOVAKIA

Constitution (Article 5)

Act of 8 July 1959 respecting the status of works committees of the basic organisations of the Revolutionary Trade Union Movement (section 1)

Labour Code, 1965, as amended by Act of 18 December 1969 to amend and supplement the Labour Code (sections 1, 18-20)

DOMINICA

Trade Unions and Trade Disputes Ordinance, 1952, as amended (section 7)

DOMINICAN REPUBLIC

Act No. 2920 of 11 June 1951 to promulgate the Labour Code (section 302)

Resolution No. 15, 1964

ECUADOR

Labour Code: Consolidation prepared by the Law Commission in force
        from 7 June 1971 (sections 205-208, 421, 428)

Civil Service Act (section 10)

EGYPT

Labour Code, 1959, as amended by Presidential Decree No. 62, 1964
        (sections 160, 162, 169, 182, 183)

EL SALVADOR

Labour Code, 1972 (sections 211, 257, 264, 266, 270, 271, 295)

ETHIOPIA

Labour Relations Proclamation No. 64, 1975 (sections 2, 49, 51)

FRANCE

Act No. 73-4 of 2 January 1973 respecting the Labour Code   (sections
        L.133-1 and 2 and L.411-2)

GABON

Act No. 88/61 of 4 January 1962 to establish the Labour Code of the
        Gabon Republic (section 4)

Draft Labour Code, 1974 (section 165)

GUATEMALA

Decree No. 1441 of 5 May 1961 to promulgate the consolidated text of
        the Labour Code, as amended (section 211, 212, 216)

GUINEA

Act No. 1/AN/60 of 30 June 1960 to establish the Labour Code of the
        Republic of Guinea (section 5)

HONDURAS

Decree No. 189 of 1 June 1959 to promulgate a Labour Code (sections
        54, 471, 472)

HONG KONG

Trade Unions Ordinance, Ch. 322 (section 55)

INDIA

Indian Trade Unions Act, 1926, as amended (section 4)

INDONESIA

Ministerial Regulation No. PER-PI/Men/1975 (sections 1-3)

IRAN

Regulations for the establishment and registration of labour organisations of 23 October 1974 (sections 22, 23, 24)

IRAQ

Labour Code: Law No. 151 of 16 July 1970 (sections 197, 198, 227, 233, 238)

IVORY COAST

Act No. 64-290 of 1 August 1964 to establish a Labour Code (section 4)

JAMAICA

Labour Relations and Industrial Disputes Act, 1975 (section 5)

JAPAN

Act No. 174 of 1 June 1949: Trade Union Law, as amended (sections 2, 5, 7)

National Public Service Act, 1965, as amended (section 108)

Local Public Service Act, 1965, as amended (section 52-54)

Rule No. 17 of 9 July 1966 of the National Personnel Authority

JORDAN

Law No. 21 of 14 May 1960 to promulgate the Labour Code (sections 1, 69)

Provisional Law No. 7 amending the Labour Code, 1960 (section 2)

KENYA

Trade Unions Ordinance, 1952 (sections 16, 18)

KUWAIT

Ordinance No. 38 of 1964 respecting labour in the private sector, as
    amended (sections 70, 71, 79, 80)

LIBERIA

Labour Practices Act, as amended (sections 4601-A, 4700)

LIBYAN ARAB JAMAHIRIYA

Act No. 58-2970 of 1 May 1970: Labour Code (sections 115, 116, 136,
    137)

MADAGASCAR

Ordinance No. 75-C13 DM of 17 May 1975 to promulgate a Labour Code
    (section 5)

MALAWI

Trade Unions Ordinance: Ch. 87 of the Laws of Nyasaland revised to
    6 February 1963, as amended (sections 17-19)

MALAYSIA

Trade Unions Ordinance (Malaya) No. 23, 1959 (sections 2, 10, 17,
    72, 73)

Trade Unions Act No. 81, 1965 (sections 2-4)

Trade Unions (Exemption of Public Officers) Order, 1967 (section 3)

Essential (Industrial Relations) Regulations, 1969

Industrial Relations Act, 1967, as amended by Industrial Relations
    (Amendment) Act, 1975 (section 5)

MAURITANIA

Labour Code, 1963, as amended by Act No. 70-030 of 23 January 1970
    (Book III, sections 1, 6)

MEXICO

Federal Law for Workers in the Service of the State, 1963 (sections
    7-71, 73, 79, 82)

Federal Labour Act, 1969 (sections 360, 363, 386-389, 395)

NEW ZEALAND

Industrial Relations Act, 1973 (sections 98-107)

NICARAGUA

Labour Code, 1945, as amended (section 9)

Trade Union Regulations, 1960 (sections 8, 43, 62)

NIGERIA

Trade Unions Decree No. 31 of 23 July 1973 (sections 1, 2, 5, 22, 23, 28, 33)

NORWAY

Act of 18 July 1958 (section 3)

PAKISTAN

Notification No. 6/1/48 ESTS (SE) of 30 August 1948

Government Servants' (Conduct) Rules, 1964 (Rule No. 28)

Industrial Relations Ordinance, 1969, as amended by Ordinance No. 29, 1973 (sections 15, 22)

Labour Relations (Amendment) Ordinance, 1975

Government Servants (Staff Relations) Ordinance (section 15) (not yet in effect at the time of preparation of this study)

PANAMA

Decree No. 252 of 30 December 1971: Labour Code (sections 344, 346)

PARAGUAY

Act No. 729 of 31 August 1961 to promulgate the Labour Code (section 289)

PERU

Supreme Decree No. 009 of 1961, as amended by Supreme Decree No. 021 of 1962 (sections 11, 23)

Civil Service Law No. 11377

PHILIPPINES

Labor Code of the Philippines, 1974, as amended by Presidential
    Decrees 570-A of 1974, and 626 and 643 of 1975 (sections 233,
    236, 237, 242, 245, 247, 248)

POLAND

Act of 1 July 1949 respecting trade unions (sections 3-9)

Labour Code, 1974 (section 20)

PORTUGAL

Legislative Decree No. 215-A

Legislative Decree No. 215-B/75 of 30 April 1975 (sections 7, 9, 11,
    12)

Resolution of the Council of Ministers of 30 September 1976

SENEGAL

Act No. 61-34 of 15 June 1961 to establish a Labour Code (section 5)

SINGAPORE

Trade Unions Ordinance, 1941, as amended by Trade Unions (Amendment)
    Act, 1967 (sections 3, 9, 29)

Industrial Relations Ordinance, 1960, as amended by Industrial
    Relations (Amendment) Act, 1968 (sections 16, 77)

Trade Unions Act, 1970 (sections 14, 15, 17)

SOMALIA

Law No. 65 of 18 October 1972: Labour Code (section 10)

REPUBLIC OF SOUTH AFRICA

Bantu Labour (Settlement of Disputes) Act, 1953

Industrial Conciliation Act, 1956 (sections 1, 5, 66, 78)

Industrial Conciliation Amendment Act, 1959

Bantu Labour Relations (Amendment) Act, 1973

SOUTHERN RHODESIA

Industrial Conciliation Act, 1959

SPAIN

Act No. 2 of 17 February 1971: Trade Union Act

Act No. 19 of 1 April 1977 to make regulations relating to trade
    union law

SRI LANKA

Trade Unions Ordinance (Ch. 138 of the Legislative Enactments of
    Ceylon, 1956 Revision, Vol. V), as amended by Acts Nos. 18 of
    1958 and 24 of 1970 (sections 3, 8)

SUDAN

Workers' Trade Unions Act, 1971 (section 9)

SWEDEN

Freedom of Association Act No. 506 of 11 September 1936, as amended
    by Act No. 332 of 17 May 1940 concerning the right of
    association (section 3)

SWITZERLAND

Federal Act of 30 June 1927 - 24 June 1949 respecting the conditions
    of service of federal employees (section 13)

Federal Act No. 55, 1956 (and decisions of the Federal Tribunal)

SYRIAN ARAB REPUBLIC

Legislative Decree No. 84 of 26 June 1968 respecting the
    organisation of trade unions (sections 2-7)

TANZANIA

National Union of Tanganyika Workers (Establishment) Act, 1964
    (sections 3, 5, 6, 12, 13)

THAILAND

Labour Relations Act, BE2518 of 14 February 1975 (sections 88, 95,
    113)

TOGO

Ordinance No. 16 of 8 May 1974: Labour Code (section 4)

TRINIDAD AND TOBAGO

Civil Service Act, 1965 (section 24)

Fire Service Act, 1965 (section 28)

Prison Service Act, 1965 (section 26)

Education Act, 1966 (section 72)

Industrial Relations Act, 1972 (sections 33-35, 5A, 71-75)

TUNISIA

Act No. 66-27 of 30 April 1966 to promulgate a Labour Code (section 242)

TURKEY

Constitution (Articles 46, 119)

Act No. 275 respecting labour agreements, 1963 (sections 7, 8)

Act No. 1317, 1970, amending and supplementing Act No. 274 respecting trade unions, 1963 (sections 1, 9)

UGANDA

Trade Unions Act, 1970, as amended by Trade Unions Act (Amendment) Decree, 1973 (sections 1, 9, 11, 15, 16)

USSR

Regulations respecting the Rights of Factory, Works and Local Trade Union Committee, 1971

Labour Code of the RSFSR (sections 7, 230)

Ukrainian SSR Labour Code, 1971 (sections 10, 14, 246, 247)

UNITED KINGDOM

Race Relations Act, 1968

Industrial Relations Act, 1971, as amended by Trade Unions and Labour Relations Act, 1974, as amended by Trade Unions and Labour Relations (Amendment) Act, 1976

Industrial Relations Code of Practice, 1972

Employment Protection Act, 1975

UNITED STATES

National Labor Relations Act, 1935, as amended by Labor Management Relations Act, 1947, as amended (sections 3, 7-9)

Act of 22 October 1951, Ch. 534, 65 Stat. 601 (sections 7, 8, 9, 14)

Civil Rights Act, 1966 (section 703)

URUGUAY

Decree No. 622/973, 1973 (section 2)

VENEZUELA

Decree No. 585 of 28 April 1971 to issue regulations respecting civil service unions (sections 7, 8)

ZAMBIA

Industrial Relations Act No. 36, 1971 (sections 5, 7, 26)

Article 1

Each Member of the International Labour Organisation for which this Convention is in force undertakes to give effect to the following provisions.

Article 2

Workers and employers, without distinction whatsoever, shall have the right to establish and, subject only to the rules of the organisation concerned, to join organisations of their own choosing without previous authorisation.

Article 3

1.   Workers' and employers' organisations shall have the right to draw up their constitutions and rules, to elect their representatives in full freedom, to organise their administration and activities and to formulate their programmes.

2.   The public authorities shall refrain from any interference which would restrict this right or impede the lawful exercise thereof.

Article 4

Workers' and employers' organisations shall not be liable to be dissolved or suspended by administrative authority.

Article 5

Workers' and employers' organisations shall have the right to establish and join federations and confederations and any such organisation, federation or confederation shall have the right to affiliate with international organisations of workers and employers.

Article 6

The provisions of Articles 2, 3 and 4 hereof apply to federations and confederations of workers' and employers' organisations.

Article 7

The acquisition of legal personality by workers' and employers' organisations, federations and confederations shall not be made subject to conditions of such a character as to restrict the application of the provisions of Articles 2, 3 and 4 hereof.

Article 8

1.   In exercising the rights provided for in this Convention workers and employers and their respective organisations, like other persons or organised collectivities, shall respect the law of the land.

2.   The law of the land shall not be such as to impair, nor shall it be so applied as to impair, the guarantees provided for in this Convention.

Article 9

1.   The extent to which the guarantees provided for in this Convention shall apply to the armed forces and the police shall be determined by national laws or regulations.

2.   In accordance with the principle set forth in paragraph 8 of article 19 of the Constitution of the International Labour Organisation the ratification of this Convention by any Member shall not be deemed to affect any existing law, award, custom or agreement in virtue of which members of the armed forces or the police enjoy any right guaranteed by this Convention.

Article 10

In this Convention the term "organisation" means any organisation of workers or of employers for furthering and defending the interests of workers or of employers.

Article 11

Each Member of the International Labour Organisation for which this Convention is in force undertakes to take all necessary and appropriate measures to ensure that workers and employers may exercise freely the right to organise.